COLLEGE STRAIGHT AHEAD

. . . .

SECRETS TO GETTING YOUR CHILD OFF TO COLLEGE WITH MINIMUM STRESS, MAXIMUM EFFICIENCY AND A CLOSE EYE ON FINANCES

Allison Golinkin
Elizabeth Labanowski
Debra Friedkin

with **Tom Morris, Ph.D.**
Bestselling author of *The Art of Achievement* and
If Aristotle Ran General Motors

TABLE OF CONTENTS

FOREWORD
Tom Morris

Everyone who is sending a child off to college needs this book. I wish it had been available years ago. If you're a parent about to launch a bird from the nest, you'll be very glad it's available now. It can help make a complex, challenging process easily manageable, and maybe even fun.

This little guide is packed full of information and advice that any college bound high school senior can use and every parent of such a student will be thankful to have. It's a valuable How-To Manual for the move to a new college or university home. In fact, it can be read with great profit by even sophomores and juniors looking ahead to college visits and the entire application process. There's one chapter devoted to campus visits, and lots of insight throughout the book can help you make the right decision about where you should apply. As both a parent and a former professor who long taught students who were new to a major campus, I have a deep appreciation for how useful this book can be.

I had the privilege of welcoming freshmen to campus for most of the fifteen years that I taught at The University of Notre Dame. As they sat among a sea of fellow newcomers on the first day of class, at the opening of the fall semester, in Philosophy 101, I could see a mixture of eagerness and uncertainty on their faces. They had come from all over the country, and from many other parts of the world. Their futures would turn on what was to happen during their time on campus. They had all successfully made the sometimes long journey from home to dorm, and now it was my job to help start them on the rest of their academic adventure well.

On that first day of classes, I could already see tired faces in the room. Some of them had arrived in town a bit unprepared for the work it would take to get fully set up in their student homes and find their way around this new community. A few long days and late nights had preceded their introduction to me, and Socrates, and Plato, and Aristotle. Most of my new students had moved to South Bend with the help of family and friends whose life experience, sharp minds, and strong arms had assisted greatly in their relocation to a new academic life. Yet, still, they all encountered a variety of unexpected challenges and obstacles long before tackling the wisdom of the ages in a classroom. The transitions from their hometowns to this new environment had often been full of surprises, unanticipated problems, and creative problem solving that would have made any great thinker proud. They had packed and shipped and picked up and unpacked and put up and organized and run all around campus looking for answers to all their what, where and how questions. They had chased down leads and found the information they needed, despite false starts, dead ends, and new twists along the way. They had finally gotten their bearings. And they had accomplished enough to make it to my class, alert, well clothed, and with notebooks in their hands. But none of this had come easily.

I know now that my new students each year and their supportive families would have benefited greatly from a chance to sit down months in advance of their move to campus and talk with Debra Friedkin, Allison Golinkin, and Elizabeth Labanowski. These three ladies have mastered the art of moving a student to a new academic environment efficiently, effectively, and happily. They all experienced personally the battle of the First College Move with an oldest child. They faced the chaos, overcame it, and finally mastered it. In this book, you have their accumulated wisdom on how do to it well yourself.

If your child is a senior in high school and has plans for college, read this book now! If you have a sophomore or junior contemplating college, you'll get a valuable head start on the process by consulting the entire book, and especially the chapter on campus visits. It will save you time, trouble, worry, and needless friction. It may even save your sanity. It will also likely save you money that's equivalent to many, many times its cost. But that will be true only if you read it thoroughly and use it well. This compendium of crucial information is a wonderful tool to help you make a smooth transition possible for your child going off to school. An exciting process awaits you, and with the advice of this book, I see great success in your future, and in your child's.

INTRODUCTION

Before anything else, preparation
is the key to success.
Alexander Graham Bell

Parents have been sending their kids off to college for many generations. They've managed it largely without formal guides or extensive help, and the students have eventually adapted just fine to their new environments. But this doesn't mean that a little help with the process along the way would have been unwelcome. In fact, the right help at the right time can make a big difference. Why muddle through this important transition when you can master it instead?

We, the authors of this book, learned this the hard way. We didn't know what we didn't know when we sent our oldest children off to college. And, boy, were we in for some surprises! In response to everything we learned through our own perplexity and problem solving, panic and quick thinking, as well as trial and error (and, believe us, there were lots of trials, along with many errors), we wrote this book to help guide other parents through it all. The result is a practical manual full of great tips and hard-won advice that we wish someone had given us in advance.

In the chapters that follow, we'll help you get your child ready, moved, and settled into college, prepared from Day One to launch this new stage of their lives. The guidance we have for you here is tried and true. It will give you a rare sense of peace and confidence during what can otherwise be a confusing and stressful process.

We were lucky. When our own oldest children were preparing to go off to school, we had the time to tackle all the problems that naturally arise during this important period of change. Not every parent does. Work schedules are demanding. Commitments are many. There are only so many hours in the day. By sharing with you what we have learned, and giving you the tools to ask all the right questions, we can help you cut dramatically the time it will take to succeed in this challenge.

We've talked with a small army of friends about what we three experienced and learned in this extended process of sending a child off to college, and we've been gratified to see our stories and insights reflected and confirmed in their own tales. We're going to be giving you a universal framework for what you face. Of course, your path will have its own twists and turns, and inevitably some craziness that maybe no one else has ever experienced. But from what we have compiled here, you'll be prepared for anything that comes. We guarantee it!

****

You may wonder if you need an entire book of advice on all this. You do. Trust us. Things have changed a lot since you were in high school. Back then, when you were applying to college, you probably sent out applications to only a few places and, likely, your parents weren't even involved in the process, except by asking now and then how it was going. Today, parenting college-bound children is vastly different, even for those of us who aren't "helicopter parents" at all, and keep our feet firmly planted on the ground. Beginning in the ninth grade of our children's educations, we're now strongly encouraged to participate actively in the college preparation journey. And we do. For the next four years, we help plan, we encourage, and we sacrifice to help ensure that our child's college dreams are realized.

Once this has all played out in your own family and your student has a college acceptance letter, or even several such letters, in hand, it's time to celebrate! Something of real importance has been achieved. And you, as a parent, have played a great supporting role. Together, you should savor the accomplishment and experience the satisfaction of this long family journey well taken.

But is your job then done? We're here to tell you that it's not. Getting your son or daughter ready for the first day of college is the next big challenge.

Leaving the comforts of home and launching out into a new world of learning is a seminal moment in life and even, in some form, a universal experience. As with any major life transition, there are countless things to be accomplished on the road to relocation. With careful planning, the result will be a smooth move, a student ready to hit the ground running, and parents who may be tired but happy, and thoroughly at ease in the knowledge that their child is ready for this new adventure. That is the promise of this book.

As you first read through all the details of our little manual, you may at first experience a feeling of being a bit overwhelmed at everything that's involved with this upcoming move. You can even feel a mild bit of inner panic. You've never done this before! But don't worry. We have. And we're here to help you help your child. You're already more of an expert on all these matters than your child is, just from your own general life experience, and we're going to raise your expertise to an entirely new level! Before you know it, you'll be an expert guide, the ideal sherpa of shopping and preparation that your child will need. As inexperienced as you may feel about all this, remember that your overall life preparation can be of great use in helping you lead your child through the process. And your child will benefit. No matter how slow you might feel getting out of the starting gate, you can make a difference. There is an old saying: "What does a snail say while riding on the back of a turtle? Wheeeeee!!!!!!!!"

We fully realize and agree completely that achieving personal independence is an important goal for students as the college years begin. But proper preparation allows successful separation on the part of everyone involved. Once parents drop their children off at college, it's time to step back and allow them to be on their own. You're always available

for advice, of course, and reassurance along the way, but your primary role has then changed.

Having your student well settled and prepared for this next chapter of life will be a source of great comfort for you both as you hug good-bye, and it will set you up for a happy next greeting as well. It will provide a strong start for the next stage of success that your child so well deserves.

CHAPTER 1

YOUR STUDENT IS IN – NOW WHAT?

The best way to predict the future
is to invent it.
Alan Kay

It's finally happened! After four years of hard work, college preparation, applications, recommendations, endless speculations, and hope, your child has finally been accepted into a program where a new and exciting adventure of higher education will take place. Now what?

First, remember the old saying, "Be careful what you wish for – you might get it." A great prize has been won, a well-deserved reward for all the hard work of the past. But to claim this prize, another extended burst of hard work lies yet ahead.

From the day the letter of acceptance arrives to the moment your child sits down in that first college class, a lot of preparation has to be accomplished. And the quality of that preparation will contribute importantly to the quality of the initial educational and social experiences to come.

You may at first feel that the road to Move-In day will surely be relatively easy – a simple exercise of looking around the house, boxing or packing up what will be needed, and getting it to campus. In reality, the process of moving to college, becoming settled and ready to hit the ground running is an arduous challenge, especially if done right. The success of your preparation will have broad consequences. How a student starts the college experience can have a major impact on how he or she feels about the school and the decision to attend. Anything you can do to smooth this transition will pay off royally in the days, weeks, months, and even years to come.

While *getting in* to college is the first crucial hurdle of higher education, *settling in* properly to get the work done well is the ultimate goal. The more prepared and organized a student is on Freshman Move-In Day, the more successful he or she will be in transitioning into this new environment. So, let's start preparing now.

✳✳✳✳✳✳✳

Getting off to college can be daunting, but take comfort in knowing that this task is a universal experience for rising scholars. The exact methodology of executing the move varies from family to family, but there are some basics that are, well, universal. How do we know? Your authors are three ordinary moms from the middle of America who had college-bound freshmen headed to different schools on different coasts located in a variety of different communities. We each had our own plan, which we executed in our own personal way. However, when the dust had settled and our children were well ensconced in their new college homes, we all shared a few cups of coffee together and relived our experiences. In regaling each other with our individual tales, we found them to be surprisingly similar.

We learned that each of our experiences had been chaotic, disorganized in some or all phases, and in many ways disappointing, because our execution of this important move did not match our expectations. Why had we gone through such problems? What should we have known that we didn't know?

As we talked about our missteps, we all wished that we had been guided through the surprising maze of creating a smooth transition to college. We felt that our hard-won, collective "wisdom" could perhaps be of value to other parents weaving their way through their own maze. If you could learn from our mistakes, you wouldn't have to make so many yourself! And so, this book!

This is your ultimate "how-to-get-it-done-with-the-least-amount-of-hassle" guide. Our easy-to-use manual is replete with questions and information that we hope will prevent you from having to reinvent the wheel that kept rolling over the three of us as we traveled our own paths. We've been to the front lines and we know what you'll need there.

You are about to face a lot of personal unknowns. And this can produce unnecessary anxiety, even great stress. You know that the more you are clued in, the easier it will be to get what you want — and not just the material items needed for the new environment, but a real enjoyment of the broader experience, along with a sense of happiness and confidence on the part of your child that will help him or her launch this new journey well. To guide you through this process, we'll clue you in on what questions you need to have answered, when you need the answers, what things you should have for the new college home, and how to get everything to the right place at the right time with your sanity at least mostly intact. We'll do all this in the form of a simple usable "how-to" manual. Understanding the broader significance of the college transition for a family, we'll equally seek to help you manage your expectations for the impending emotional rollercoaster, as your child leaves one nest to feather a new one.

This book is written to be your action plan for preparing your child for college. It's like a big checklist, with explanations. As airline pilots, hospital emergency room staffs, and military personnel have come to understand, along with many parents of college bound students, a well-designed checklist can make all the difference between success and failure in any crucial task.

This book is purposely divided into chapters and sections to help you break the process down into manageable pieces. The work of getting ready for college has many components, and many surprises, even for the most prepared of families. Once all sections of the book are completed, you will have at your fingertips a ready source of information that will continue to be a helpful reference during the four (or more – it happens!) college years to come.

****

Our friend, the philosopher Tom Morris, who graciously wrote the foreword to this book and has helped us in many ways get our thoughts onto paper, has spent over twenty years studying what the wisest people in history have had to say about attaining success in any challenging endeavor. He has identified seven universal conditions for satisfying and exemplary achievement that he likes to call "The 7 Cs of Success." They structure two of his most insightful books, *True Success* and *The Art of Achievement*, either of which would help your child to be very successful throughout the upcoming college years. During the many years that Tom taught freshmen at Notre Dame these tools of success, they most often went on to great academic accomplishments, superlative personal victories, and many even won national championships, as well as, in later life, Super Bowl rings! They are living proof that, whatever the challenge might be, wisdom can help us win! We want to spend a minute here at the outset of our time together telling you about this universal framework for success because it can help you on to championship level accomplishments in your upcoming move, and will guide you well into the ultimate success that you and your child need in this multi-faceted challenge.

The 7 C's of Success
And Your Big College Move

For True Success in any challenge, we need:

1. A clear CONCEPTION of what we want, a vivid vision, a goal clearly imagined.

You want to experience a great transition to college life, a smooth and effective Move-In Day, and to get your student set up well for every form of success that he or she will be seeking in the new educational and social environment. Vividly envision a happy new college life and then you can begin to take appropriate action to make it happen.

19

2. A strong CONFIDENCE that we can attain the goal.

You should approach any new challenge with a good measure of inner confidence. In this book, we'll give you what you need to build that confidence regarding the big move to come. We're experienced guides, and you can trust us to prepare you well. But then it's up to you. Don't venture forth worrying yourself to death in a state of trepidation and high anxiety. Have the courage and belief that you can do everything it takes, solve every problem, and think of all relevant factors to bring this off with great success!

3. A focused CONCENTRATION on what it takes to reach the goal.

It's our job to help you focus your concentration on everything it will take to reach your goal of a well-organized and appropriate transition to college. We can promise you that a properly focused concentration of thought and action will get you across the finish line in great form and ahead of the pack!

4. A stubborn CONSISTENCY in pursuing our vision.

Between now and Move-In Day, there will be plenty of temptations for procrastination. Believe us, we've felt them all. You can even be tempted to drop an important part of the preparations we suggest, thinking that maybe it's not so crucial after all. But that would be a big mistake! We want to help you to do it all right! And a big part of that is remaining consistent with your goals. Do whatever it takes to get it right. Recognize inconsistent behavior for what it is, and in the great words of Deputy Barney Fife, "Nip it in the bud!"

5. An emotional COMMITMENT to the importance of what we're doing.

In the darkest days of preparation, when you're completely exhausted and feel like you can't make another phone call, or visit another store with a shopping list in hand, remind yourself of what's at stake here: This is all about your child's successful transition to what may easily become their most important and formative environment other than their original home with you. For the student's involvement in these preparations, he or she needs to remember that all of this is vital for laying the foundations for a great time of enjoyment and achievement to come.

6. A good CHARACTER to guide us and keep us on a proper course.

To the great philosophers and diagnosticians of human nature throughout the centuries, character is all about our ability to recognize, understand, and react well to external reality, including the people around us. In this journey of preparation for the college move, you'll be asking your child many questions, and your child will be challenged to engage in self-examination (especially when it comes to potential roommate questions). Candid, open honesty in all things is a requirement. Displaying kindness, forbearance, and respect for each other is crucial. You're going to be working as a team. And teamwork requires trust, trustworthiness, a sense of humor, patience, persistence, determination, and many other

qualities of good character. The better everyone on the team works together, the better it will all go!

7. A CAPACITY TO ENJOY THE PROCESS along the way.

You have ahead of you some hard work, but there will also be many opportunities for enjoying the process. It's OK to joke around, and even tease lovingly. It's all right to laugh at absurdity! And it's important to savor your small accomplishments along the way. This process can actually bring you and your child closer together when it's done right. If you find ways to enjoy the process, and make ways to enjoy yourself throughout the process, however tedious it may sometimes seem, you'll find the ultimate results even more enjoyable as well!

Follow these seven conditions of success, use our many suggestions yet to come, and in the end, you'll be able to celebrate a very successful move!

✳✳✳✳✳✳✳

We want this book to bring you help, encouragement, insight, and even a sense of relief! If used properly, it can be both your roadmap and timetable for achieving your goal of moving your child to college with an absolute minimum of stress.

To get the most out of the book, you should do and remember these things:

- First, read this book in its entirety to better understand the full scope of the project in front of you.

- After you have read it, never let it out of your sight! Or at least: Don't leave home without it! There is ample room for notation, and just as you wouldn't begin a major trip without a guidebook, you don't want to embark on the college journey without this guide.

- This book will become an even more instrumental reference for you as you literally fill in the blanks over the next several months. You will be impressed (with yourself!) that you have amassed so much useful information. And what you accomplish as a result will help you to be a guide to friends who also face this big task, whether simultaneously, or in the future. You may even come to see how a copy of this book might make a great gift for any friend who is a parent of the college bound!

- The checklists included in each chapter have been created to include *every* possible question you will need to ask and any item that you might need or want. No stone has been left unturned.

- However you use the information in this book – in a broad-brush way or in its very specific detail – you should know that you have been made aware of the myriad questions that will make you extremely college savvy before you have even stepped onto campus for The Great Relocation.

Parents, with what you have in your hands now, consider yourselves well armed to move boldly ahead!

NOTES: _____

CHAPTER 2

MAPPING OUT THE PLAN

A goal without a plan is just a wish.
Antoine de Saint-Exupery

Once you have read through this book for the first time, you will be aware of how many "i's" there are to dot and "t's" there are to cross in planning the college transition. So your first order of business is to pull all the pieces together and develop an organized plan. In this section, our purpose is to impose order and discipline on the college send-off process by defining the milestones and setting the goals that will get you to the promised land known as Freshman Move-In Day.

Rome was not built in a day, and neither was New Haven, or Austin, Texas. Executing a plan to get ready for college will not happen overnight, either. We've taken the various tasks discussed in the following chapters and put them in order - from the general admission date in April through typical move-in dates in August, providing five months of scheduling. You can follow our calendar in this chapter, or if you are more visual, feel free to lay out these tasks in your monthly planner or create your own timeline. Your child will need to perform one task or more each month. Remember, the whole reason for this book is to avoid last-minute stress and panic. Be sure to check off items as you complete them.

If your child is an "early admit," you can jump-start the process that we have outlined below, since he or she will have made the definitive college decision several months before regular admits. We recommend that you use this lead-time to complete the tasks listed in this book, including asking preparatory questions of college officials, and even considering a visit to campus. Colleges love to work with "early admits" in January and February, before the crush of the regular admission process. Do not be shy – plunge right in and start familiarizing yourself with your child's soon-to-be college home.

****

NOTES: _____

_____

_____

_____

_____

_____

_____

_____

_____

_____

_____

_____

_____

_____

_____

_____

_____

_____

For parents of "regular admits," here is your five-month plan:

April
Where Is My Child Going to College?

This is the month for your child to figure out where he or she will spend most of the next four years. Of course, the decision may already have been made, long before the coveted letter arrives. One school may be "in the family," or may be a long-term dream. There might be a college to which your child's friends have all applied and where they're all committed. Your student may have his or her personal reasons for loving one school, one campus, or one field of study best represented at one of the colleges. Even if the place of matriculation is a foregone conclusion, there are still some questions you may need to ask, and information you may want to gather at this stage, if just to reinforce the decision and allow the family to move forward with eyes wide open.

In case there are multiple acceptances, and a decision has not been made, your help as a parent can be very useful at this stage. Even though you may want to just sit back and enjoy this moment of triumph, when two or more schools have welcomed your child, you can immediately help jump-start the process of evaluating the various institutions to which your child has been admitted. Could he or she do this alone? Sure. But you've lived long enough and have had to evaluate enough options in your life that you can be of great help at this juncture, without for a moment hovering like the classic helicopter parent and pressing your own personal views unhelpfully on your child. Your role now can be thought of as a key research assistant, sounding board, and advisor. Take it seriously, and do it well, while showing all due respect and confidence in your child's ability to make this decision appropriately! In fact, go out of your way to emphasize your esteem for your child as a decision-maker. But continue to offer your support. This decision can seem "so big" as to be a bit scary for a teen. Your proper support can help build confidence in the process and in the ultimate choice, as you utilize every available resource to help your child make the best, most informed decision possible.

Focus primarily on the question of which college is the best fit for your child. Here are some pointers.

- If finances allow, consider a visit to the campus on "admitted student" days to get a true flavor of the college and its campus culture. A phone call to the admissions office can clarify whether this is available, even if the paperwork you've received doesn't explicitly offer it as an option.

NOTES: _____

_____

_____

_____

_____

_____

_____

_____

_____

_____

_____

_____

_____

_____

_____

_____

_____

_____

- If you are unable to visit the campus, pick up your phone and call the admissions officer at each school. They have worked hard to get your child in, and they have a vested interest in having him/her attend their school. They will be glad to answer your questions. Also ask for the names and contact information of alumni in your community who have stated a willingness to advise prospective students.

- Guide your child to set up meetings with one or two of these alumni and get their honest appraisal of their experiences at the college.

- Evaluate financial aid packages.

- If your child has a learning disability, a chronic illness or other special need as a student, it is critical that you assess how responsive a college will be to those needs. Find out who is in charge of these issues on campus, make a call, and discuss the extent to which your child's needs will be accommodated. Do not just assume that your child's college will be as accommodating as his or her high school! Remember that your important family member is now one fish among a great many in a much larger pond.

- Check out the colleges to which your child has been admitted by investigating their websites *in detail*, reading evaluations in college guidebooks, etc.

- Visit social networking websites and find other students who attend these schools. Recommend that your child "friend them" and pick their brains.

With all the information that you and your child have gathered, offer to talk through the decision, and when it's made, send in your deposit by the deadline. Together, you'll feel a burden lifted, and you'll share in the excitement of anticipating the big move to come!

May
Goodbye, High School!

This is the month for your son or daughter to savor the last moments of high school, finish up on a high note, walk across stage to receive that long awaited diploma, and begin the new drive forward, only occasionally looking in the rearview mirror, but with great satisfaction for a job well done. When the caps and gowns come off, there's a new focus in front of you. After all, college is straight ahead!

NOTES: _____

_____

_____

_____

_____

_____

_____

_____

_____

_____

_____

_____

_____

_____

_____

_____

_____

_____

_____

_____

Note: Some colleges send out important packets in mid-May that require action on your part by June 1. If you receive ANYTHING from your school, open it immediately, read it carefully, and then respond in a timely fashion to any deadlines. The entire family should be on the alert for any such mailings, and should make sure they get the attention they need.

June
Hello, College!

June is all about the big push to prepare for college. With high school finally complete, here is what to expect and do in June:

- Be on the lookout for a letter or packet from your child's college detailing information and timing that is specific and pertinent for all in-coming freshmen.

  Make sure you read this information carefully, extract the critical dates and put them on your own calendar. You may be receiving, in this packet or subsequent mailings, information about roommate and dormitory preferences, orientation opportunities, freshman trips, academic testing for course placement, medical forms, insurance options, etc. Pay careful attention to each, take action as needed, and keep any mailings well organized in a single location. And, of course, be sure to respond as requested well before the due dates. Much of this information is crucial for your child being properly enrolled in the university's system. So, do not put off until tomorrow what you can do today.

- Re-examine the college's website. You will be amazed at the wealth of information available for new admits and their parents. Remember, websites are dynamic and can be a constant source of new and helpful information, so check and re-check them regularly.

  Print off the college's academic calendar. Make sure your student is familiar with it. The sense of freedom that comes from finally graduating high school can make it seem like any next academic commitment is endlessly far away, when it's actually just around the corner. Use the calendar to help impart to your child a proper sense of urgency about taking action to prepare for the upcoming move. Otherwise, you may find yourself working against the strongest summer inertia you've ever seen.

NOTES: _____

_____

_____

_____

_____

_____

_____

_____

_____

_____

_____

_____

_____

_____

_____

_____

_____

_____

_____

The calendar for the upcoming academic year will be located on either a freshman-specific page or the general college website. It contains important dates (i.e. orientation, freshman move in, parents' weekend, school holidays, move-out dates, etc.) that apply to every student. It is important that you print off the calendar, mark the dates in your personal calendar, and fill in the Critical Dates form found at the end of this book, for easy future reference.

- If it's at all possible, take a physical or virtual tour of the college campus and surrounding community (see Chapters 3 and 4 below).

It is crucial that you collect this information in June. Even if you plan a summer orientation trip to your college later on, your data gathering in June will add significant value to your trip.

- Make all of your hotel, airline/transportation and car rental reservations.

If there is a summer orientation for incoming freshmen, make your reservations (air, hotel, car) NOW. While you're at it, plan your trip for Freshman Move-In. Reserve rooms and rental cars, if needed, early, since this date applies to all the incoming freshmen, making hotel rooms scarce and sometimes making car and van rental availability even worse.

For Freshman Move-In, be sure to arrive at least two days before the actual dormitory move-in date in order to complete local shopping in preparation for the big move.

- Attend any incoming student and family functions, whether formal or informal, that might be hosted in your community.

Do not overlook the importance of networking with current students, families and alumni in your area. Their guidance and tips can be invaluable. They've been through most of what you'll go through, and they may have answers to questions you would not even otherwise think to ask. Always remember our theme song: You don't know what you don't know!

- Review the detailed discussion and shopping lists found in Chapter 7 of this book.

NOTES: _____

_____

_____

_____

_____

_____

_____

_____

_____

_____

_____

_____

_____

_____

_____

_____

_____

_____

_____

_____

Make a master list of everything your child will need to take to college. Feel free to create your own master list, or just supplement the one we have in Chapter 7. Every single item on the master list must be designated as something you already own, something you will purchase in your hometown before the move, or else something you'll purchase in your new college town. Chapter 7 will provide more detail.

July
Ready, Aim, Shop

You have completed your data gathering, reviewed our shopping lists, and created your own. July is the month to shop 'til you drop, but always with an eye on costs. You'll want to keep your radar on and your eyes peeled for bargains, as there will be plenty out there. Be sure to take your list with you everywhere, so that you can refer to it often. Just remember: You're lost without the list.

Budget enough time to be able to shop at a leisurely pace (and therefore, wisely and creatively). You will find that many retailers use July as the month to promote back-to-school and off-to-college sales. Take advantage of well-stocked stores that will be teeming with items you need. If you wait until August, you will be disappointed, as many goods become out of stock and unavailable.

July is also typically the month when colleges issue dorm and roommate assignments. If that is the case for your child, be sure that he or she gets in touch with the new roommate before you shop, to avoid unneeded duplication of things being bought or brought. It's especially important to distribute the task of purchasing larger items such as a TV, microwave, fridge, or sofa.

Here are some shopping tips:

- Make a list of the major retailers in your area that stock the items on your list.

  Review our list of recommended major retailers in Chapter 7 and supplement that list with your local and online favorites.

- Be on the lookout for specials, coupons, and catalogues from the stores you will be frequenting.

  Check out the Sunday newspaper circulars from stores like Home Depot, Lowe's, and Best Buy, which contain numerous specials on items you will need. Compare local pricing to what's available online or offered by your college bookstore.

NOTES: _____

_____

_____

_____

_____

_____

_____

_____

_____

_____

_____

_____

_____

_____

_____

_____

_____

_____

- Don't overlook clothes shopping.

  This is a great time for your son or daughter to refresh and add to their wardrobe, because just about everything is on sale.

- Designate a single place in your house where ALL off-to-college purchases and gear will be kept until they are packed.

Here's the happy paradox you face: In order to bring all this off well, you're going to need an almost military sense of discipline, combined with a spirit of celebratory anticipation. That's right: Celebratory anticipation. There can be an element of fun in all this, and there should be, when done right. After all, this isn't meant to be a relentless death march through every big box retailer you can find. It's not your own personal retail version of The Trail of Tears. It's preparation for something great! But it's also something whose preparation should be equally great. And that takes organization!

August
College, Here We Come

This month is all about getting ready for the big move and tying up loose ends. Here is what to focus on:

- Review the information you acquired while data gathering back in June.

  Refer to your notes in Chapters 3 and 4. Be sure you have completed all items on the list that required action, such as opening a bank account.

- If you will need to ship items to school, make a final determination of what you will pack and take with you versus what you will ship.

- Choose a shipper.

- Determine the date by which any shipped packages must be sent in order for them to arrive before you do.

- Complete any online ordering.

- Be sure that you schedule your orders and other shipments to arrive at your chosen shipping destination before you do. It's always better for them to await you than for you to be waiting for them. Boxes have nothing else to do. You will.

NOTES: _____

_____

_____

_____

_____

_____

_____

_____

_____

_____

_____

_____

_____

_____

_____

_____

_____

_____

_____

- Pack your duffels or suitcases in line with the recommendations in Chapter 8.

- Attend send-off receptions in your hometown.

- Call your college if you have ANY questions about Move-In Day. This is one of those wonderful times in life where no question is a dumb question.

- BIG TIP: As a family, develop a Move-In Day action plan. See Chapter 9 for more detail.

Now, take a deep cleansing breath. College excitement is straight ahead.

NOTES: _____

_____

_____

_____

_____

_____

_____

_____

_____

_____

_____

_____

_____

_____

_____

_____

_____

_____

CHAPTER 3

DATA GATHERING – THE CAMPUS

The next best thing to knowing something
is knowing where to find it.
Samuel Johnson

You may not realize it, but you and your child are already professionals at accomplishing the first critical step of developing an action plan – data gathering. For the past four years, you have been searching for any clues or advice that would give you an inside edge in achieving your child's goal of getting into a college of choice. Now is the time to apply your sharply honed skills to sleuthing out every possible bit of information about the college, securing an informational advantage once again.

Make no mistake: The information you accumulated during the process of assessing 'best fit' in the college search process is vastly different from the information you now need to gather in order to make your child's new college and its community feel like home.

As you consider what needs to be accomplished over the next few months, you may wonder why we feel that data gathering is so important. After all, isn't moving to college just a matter of buying some sheets and towels and packing a suitcase? In short, NO! Your son or daughter is moving to a completely new environment. In order for them to hit the ground running and feel comfortable with this new home, they need to arrive with knowledge, knowledge, and more knowledge.

The best way to obtain that knowledge is to re-visit the college – either in person or electronically – but this time, with a different perspective than you held during the college research days. To guide your new search for answers, we have provided dozens of questions that you and your child would be wise to ask, ranging from concerns about residential life to technology and book buying. They are written in the first person, with the hope that your child will be asking at least some of them. However, remembering the limits of our own children's bandwidth before leaving for college, we understand there's an excellent chance that you, the parent, may end up tackling the majority of this task of data gathering.

And that's ok, too. But it should be a shared adventure, as much as possible. Regardless of how you divide the responsibility of asking these questions, they must all be addressed, and you and your child should discuss them thoroughly so that both of you approach the college move-in process armed with relevant and helpful information.

NOTES: _____

_____

_____

_____

_____

_____

_____

_____

_____

_____

_____

_____

_____

_____

_____

_____

_____

_____

_____

Keep in mind that if you speak to someone face-to-face on campus, it may be awkward to methodically read through the questions we've listed. In fact, you may find greater success with a less structured conversation, asking some preliminary questions and then letting the conversation develop naturally. If after that conversation there are still unanswered questions, make it known and, if appropriate, ask if another departmental representative would be available to assist. If not, don't panic. A follow-up phone conversation can always be scheduled at a convenient later time. Regardless of how you or your child makes contact, remember to ask to be connected with someone who has sufficient knowledge and time to answer your questions.

✳✳✳✳✳✳✳

As your family engages in the data gathering process, keep in mind that wonderful nuggets of information will come to you from places you least expect! And we don't mean fortune cookies, Ouija Boards, psychics, or Crazy Eight Balls – although you might occasionally be tempted. For instance, you may find out about the best place to stay during campus visits from a staff member in the campus mail center on Move-In Day. Or the receptionist at the admissions office may offer great suggestions for where to find the closest pharmacy or best Italian restaurant. Your hotel desk staff will also be an invaluable source of information about your new college community. These conversations, sometimes more helpful and insightful than those you conduct officially, will often catch you by surprise. To prepare yourself, we strongly encourage that you and your child read through this book completely before following any of the suggestions we provide. After all, in order to recognize all relevant nuggets of good information when they come your way and then take proper action, you first must know what information you'll need. So, be prepared for your data gathering, but also be flexible.

We have provided a list of talking points to guide your child's conversation with each department. With a roadmap in-hand, he or she can be sure to take away the most pertinent information. We have also provided ample space for you to write down the answers they receive. If you trust that the questions we've provided are important, as you and your child ask them and receive answers, you will begin to see your action plan take shape, and you'll move one step closer to a smooth college transition. But remember, whether meeting with an official or unexpected campus representative, it's important to always have your antennae engaged, since information will not necessarily come to you in the exact order we've outlined below.

As you explore the questions we've identified as important, it's worth nothing that colleges may differ in how they name their departments, though all schools have essentially the same ones. If you're ever in doubt, call the main college telephone number and describe to the operator what information you seek. She'll most likely know the person with whom you need to speak.

NOTES: _____

_____

_____

_____

_____

_____

_____

_____

_____

_____

_____

_____

_____

_____

_____

_____

_____

_____

Now, read on... your fact-finding tour begins here:

FRESHMAN WEBSITE/
FRESHMAN DEAN'S OFFICE

Most schools have a special website for incoming freshmen that contains important dates and information. Peruse the website and make copies of any sections that have special interest to you. As we've noted already, your child will probably have received a mailing in the early summer from the Freshman Dean's Office. If you have not received it, or if you still have unanswered questions, the Freshman Dean's Office needs to be your child's next stop or phone call.

Your rising collegian should ask:

- When can I expect to receive a packet of information from this office and what will it contain? _____

    _____

- Is there one or more freshmen orientations? _____

- Do I need to register in advance? If so, when? _____

    _____

- How do I register? _____

    _____

- Is there a special orientation for parents at the same time? _____

- Do they need to register and, if yes, how and by when? _____

- Is there someone who can advise me about freshman course selection? _____
    If so, who is it, and when can I get in touch with him or her? _____

    _____

    NOTE: Stop for a minute and consider the main reason you are even going to college – to learn! So, the process of course selection and your actual registration in those courses have to be a top priority. Every school has its own method for accomplishing this. It's your task to determine how your school operates.

- When does academic testing occur? How and where do I take any required tests (e.g. on-line, during orientation, etc.)? _____

    _____

    _____

    _____

NOTES: _____

_____

_____

_____

_____

_____

_____

_____

_____

_____

_____

_____

_____

_____

_____

_____

_____

_____

_____

_____

- Do I need to register for academic testing during orientation (i.e. to determine what level of certain courses I can take)? _____
_____

- Are there any special programs before school starts that are intended for freshmen?

  - What are they? _____
  _____

  - When are they? _____
  _____

  - What are their benefits? How much do they cost? _____
  _____

  - When do I need to register? _____
  _____

- Do you have other personal questions you need answered? Never hesitate to ask! ____
_____
_____
_____

✶✶✶✶✶✶✶

RESIDENTIAL LIFE

The Residential Life department is the heartbeat of things that are nearest and dearest to students. It is the repository for information that will give you and your child a firm handle on key aspects of everyday campus life.

The list below is exhaustive (and might exhaust you just reading it!), but don't despair. Your contact in the Housing Department will have been asked and will have answered these and other questions a million times, and will be able to deal with them quickly. So don't be shy—ask away!

If you are visiting, don't forget a camera and a measuring tape so that when you ask to see some dorm rooms (and you should!), you will be properly armed to make the most of your visit. If you are not able to visit in person, ask your virtual contact if the college's website has dorm floor plans that you can reference as you talk. We have organized the list of

NOTES:

questions for you by topic, to enable you and your child to keep the conversation focused, and moving efficiently and smoothly.

Dorm Rooms

What are the types of dorms available for freshmen?
- Freshman-only? _____
- Is Freshman housing located in a specific area? _____
- Where can I obtain a campus map that shows me where the dorms and other campus buildings are located? _____
- Are all dorms coed? _____
- If yes, are they coed by floor or mixed? _____
- Are there substance-free dorms? _____
- Are there "themed" dorms, e.g. international, etc.? _____
- How are dorms assigned? _____
- Can I state a dorm preference? _____
- What types of rooms are there, e.g. singles, suites, doubles? _____
- Can I state a room preference? _____
- If yes, what are my chances of receiving my preferences? _____
- Are there residential advisors in each dorm? _____
- If yes, do they reside on each floor and how many are there on each floor? _____
- What is the role of the residential advisor? _____

NOTES: _____

_____

_____

_____

_____

_____

_____

_____

_____

_____

_____

_____

_____

_____

_____

_____

_____

_____

_____

○   About the rooms –

TIP: If you are having a face-to-face visit, ask to see rooms in several dorms. If you are on the phone, be sure to ask if there are floor plans of the dorms online, to be referenced as you talk. When you receive your room assignment, call Residential Life and ask questions specific to the particular room you have been assigned.

- What specifically is included in the room? _____
- What size is the bed?

  Twin_____ Extra-Long _____

- What about the mattress? Will I need an "egg crate" or extra thick mattress pad to make it more comfortable? _____

  _____

- Are the beds bunked? _____
- Can they be un-bunked? _____
- Do the beds "loft" (i.e. can they be raised so you can put items underneath, like extra drawer units)?

  _____

  - If yes, what is the height from the floor to the bottom of the bed when lofted?

    _____

  - Does the school provide a "lofting kit?"

    _____

- Are the rooms carpeted? _____
- If not, is there a source on campus for cut-to-fit carpeting for my room?

  _____

- What about the desk?
  - Size _____
  - Number of drawers _____
  - Are there shelves above the bookcase, and if, so, how many?

    _____

- Is there a closet? If so, what are the dimensions? _____
- Is there a wardrobe? _____ _____
  - Dimensions_____
  - Configuration (i.e. drawers, shelves, etc.) _____

NOTES: _____

_____

_____

_____

_____

_____

_____

_____

_____

_____

_____

_____

_____

_____

_____

_____

_____

_____

_____

_____

_____

- Is there a separate dresser? _____
    - Dimensions_____
    - How many drawers? _____
- Can the room be re-arranged or is it "set" due to placement of outlets, Ethernet connection, phone jacks, etc.? _____
- Is a desk chair provided? _____
    - Can I bring one of my own? (Be sure to measure and get dimensions of kneehole space and height of desk to be certain that a chair you bring will fit). _____
- Is a desk light provided _____
    - If not, can the one I bring be halogen _____

TIP: If you are to provide your own light, be sure you know if a standard desk lamp will fit on the desk or if it will need to be a clip-on or standing lamp.

- Is a full-length mirror provided?_____
    - If not, can one be attached somewhere in the room, such as on the door of the wardrobe or closet? _____
- Are there towel bars or hooks in the room? _____

    _____

- Are there any wall shelves in the room? _____
- If so, how many? _____
- Are small refrigerators allowed in the rooms? _____
- Does the school itself provide any refrigerators? Or do I buy my own, or rent one on campus? _____
- If not provided, how large a room refrigerator (cubic ft) is allowed?_____

    _____

- Are microwaves allowed?_____
    If so, what wattage? _____
- Is cable TV available? If so, does the school provide this service, or do I arrange service for myself? _____
    Are cable cords provided? _____
- How is the internet accessed? _____
    Wi-Fi _____Ethernet _____

    _____

NOTES: _____

_____

_____

_____

_____

_____

_____

_____

_____

_____

_____

_____

_____

_____

_____

_____

_____

_____

- Are telephone landlines provided? _____
  _____

- What kind of phone jack is there? _____
  _____

- If Ethernet, cable and/or phone cords are provided, where and when do I pick them up? _____
  _____

- How many electrical outlets are there? _____
  Where are they located? _____

TIP: You will need an approximation so that you know the lengths of extension cords and how many power strips or plug adaptors you will need to bring. _____

- Is there a basin in the room? _____

Roommates

- How are they assigned? _____
  _____
  _____

- Am I able to choose my own roommate? _____
- What are the chances my preference will be honored? _____
  _____

- When will I be notified with my roommate's name? _____
  _____

- Will I be given contact information for him or her, or do we have to wait until move-in day? _____

Bathrooms

- How many bathrooms are there per floor? _____
- Do suites have separate baths? _____
- Are the bathrooms coed? _____

NOTES: _____

_____

_____

_____

_____

_____

_____

_____

_____

_____

_____

_____

_____

_____

_____

_____

_____

_____

_____

_____

Laundry Room

- Is there one per floor, every other floor, or one for the whole building? _____

  _____

- How many washers and dryers are there in each? _____

  _____

- What is the cost of using the washers/dryers? _____

  _____

- Will my campus debit card work to operate the machines or will I need coins? ____

  _____

- Is there a laundry service available to students? _____

  _____

- If so, how much does it cost? _____

  _____

Extra Storage

- Is storage available in the dorm or somewhere on campus for large suitcases/trunks? _____

  _____

- Is storage available for my items on campus between sessions or terms? _____

  _____

- If storage is not available, what are names of local personal storage facilities in the area that can be rented? _____

  _____

TIP: You might want to rent a storage unit for the entire year for storage of out-of-season clothes, or special equipment like golf clubs, as well big items you do not want to haul home over the summer like a TV or a sofa. Consider finding some other person who might want to share a space with you to defray the cost, though most small units are reasonably priced.

- How do most students handle storage of large items over the summer? _____

  _____

  _____

  _____

NOTES: _____

_____

_____

_____

_____

_____

_____

_____

_____

_____

_____

_____

_____

_____

_____

_____

_____

_____

_____

_____

Dining/Meal Plans

TIP: Plan to visit and eat in a dining hall if you are on campus.

- Is there a required Freshman meal plan? If so, please describe it. _____

  _____

- If not, what are my other meal plan options? _____

  _____

- What are the fees for the various plans? _____

  _____

- How many on-campus dining locations are there?_____

  _____

- What are they (dining hall, coffee shop, student center, etc.)? _____

  _____

Campus Debit Cards

- Does my college use one? _____

  _____

- How does it work? _____

  _____

- What does it cover/where can it be used? _____

  _____

Transportation Around Campus

- How do I get around campus? _____

  _____

- Is there a shuttle bus? If yes, does it only make campus stops or does it also make trips off campus (if so, where)? _____

  _____

- Are bikes commonly used on campus and in town? If yes, where do I rent or buy one? _____

  _____

- Does a bike need a permit sticker? If so, where do I get one? _____

  _____

- Is special transportation service available to local airports during holiday times/spring break? _____

  _____

- Can freshmen have cars? If so, what percentage of freshmen have one? _____

  _____

NOTES: _____

_____

_____

_____

_____

_____

_____

_____

_____

_____

_____

_____

_____

_____

_____

_____

_____

_____

_____

_____

- How is parking allocated? _____

_____

- Are there special rules pertaining to having a car? _____

_____

Religious Services

- Are regular religious services held on campus? _____
- Are they non-denominational only?_____
- If not, where and when are denomination-specific services held? _____

_____

- What religious groups are represented on campus (i.e. Campus Crusade for Christ, Hillel, etc.)?_____

_____

- Are there individual student centers for various faiths?_____

_____

- Where do I get more information about them? _____

_____

Freshman Move-In Day

TIP: Get a detailed description of how the day is structured and what exactly can be expected. This is CRITICAL. Make your hotel reservations IMMEDIATELY, as every other incoming freshman and their family will also need a reservation and you could be left roomless. Also, do not forget to reserve your rental car early, and be sure to secure a BIG car or van for transporting all of your child's stuff to your new dorm. If you are coming from a significant distance and will have shipped packages, we recommend that you arrive a few days early in order to pick up your packages and complete your pre move-in shopping.

- What is the exact date that freshmen are allowed to move into their dorm rooms?

_____

- What are the specific names of recommended local hotels/motels?_____

_____

_____

_____

- Where can I find a detailed schedule covering freshmen move-in activities for students and parents?_____

_____

NOTES: _____

_____

_____

_____

_____

_____

_____

_____

_____

_____

_____

_____

_____

_____

_____

_____

_____

_____

TIP: Move-in Day is difficult at best. See our detailed discussion in Chapter 9. It is tiring, stressful and emotional for students and parents, alike. GET THE FACTS about what to expect, and you can minimize the emotional wear and tear on everyone.

By this time, even though your child may want to get off the phone, he or she should hang on for a few more minutes in order to maximize the information you both receive from your contact. Remember, the person on the other side of the phone is a local in your child's soon-to-be-new community, and likely possesses pearls of wisdom outside the confines of official college business. So while the conversation is flowing, your son or daughter should ask:

- Where do students shop for groceries? _____

  _____

- Where is a good place to shop for drug store kind of supplies? _____

  _____

- Is/are there nearby retail shopping center(s)? If so, where? _____

  Is there a Wal-Mart, Target or similar "big-box" store close by? Where? _____

  _____

  _____

  _____

- What's the most "student friendly" bank in town with convenient ATM?

  _____

- What are the best places in or around your new college for parents to stay? _____

  _____

  _____

- What are some popular area restaurants?

  _____

  _____

  _____

  _____

COMPLETE:_____

Are you tired after reading this? Do you still think that your child's move to college is just about a bag of clothes, some sheets and towels? Or do you wish this were true? Don't despair! The end is in sight!

NOTES: _____

_____

_____

_____

_____

_____

_____

_____

_____

_____

_____

_____

_____

_____

_____

_____

_____

_____

_____

The good news is that once you have all of these questions answered, you will be on a well deserved "high" with all of your newfound knowledge. Knowledge truly is power, and with every bit of new information, your family will feel less apprehensive about the impending move and more excited about the new life that awaits. So read on...

✱✱✱✱✱✱✱

THE COLLEGE MAIL CENTER

Finding out the policies of your school's Mail Center will be very important to the execution of your overall plan. Some Mail Centers will allow students to send packages addressed to themselves in advance of arriving on campus. Others will not allow mail to arrive prior to your arrival. Still other Mail Centers place a limit on the number of packages you can send from home for move-in day.

If you are making a campus visit, by all means, drop by the Mail Center, or if you are gathering your information by phone, be sure to dial its extension. Your child will want to ask:

Mail Center Procedures

- Will I be assigned a personal mailbox number? If so, how and when? _____

  _____

- How exactly should a letter or package be addressed to me? _____

  _____

- Will my address be the same for all 4 years? _____
- Can I send packages/boxes to get here PRIOR to my arrival on campus? _____

  _____

- If yes, what is the earliest date that the mail center will receive them and is there a limit to the number I can send? _____

  _____

- If no, then where can I have them sent (post office box, hotel, held by third party carrier)? _____

  _____

- If I'm allowed to send boxes prior to my arrival, can I pick them up before move-in day? _____

- What are the hours of operation of the Mail Center? _____

NOTES: _____

_____

_____

_____

_____

_____

_____

_____

_____

_____

_____

_____

_____

_____

_____

_____

_____

_____

_____

_____

Mail Center Resources

- Can I mail letters and packages from this location? _____
  _____

- If yes, what methods of mailing/shipment are available for me to use (US Mail, UPS, FEDEX, etc.)? _____
  _____

- How am I notified (once I'm on campus) if I receive a package, (e.g. by e-mail, a notice in my mailbox)? _____
  _____

- What time of day is mail received and what time is it available for pick-up?
  _____

******

THE HEALTH CENTER

Expect the best – but also always prepare for the worst! Isn't that how the old adage goes? Well, your college's Health Center falls into this category. All colleges have professionally staffed Health Centers on campus. This is an important stop on your "tour" because health situations and crises do occasionally occur and not only during normal business hours. When it's 11:00 on a Saturday night and your son or daughter is in need of medical help, your child and you will want to know how the Health Center operates! To prepare for the unexpected, your student should collect all health-related logistical information up-front.

We all hope and expect that this will be a seldom-used resource during your child's college days, but inevitably, medical needs will arise that compel your child to visit the Health Center. It is critical that you know how your college's Health Center functions, especially if your child has a chronic health problem.

If your family is paying a physical visit to campus, stop in and introduce yourselves – even ask to see the doctor or nurse in charge. The same applies to those who follow-up by phone. To best understand how the Health Center can help your child, he or she should ask:

- How does the Health Center see patients? _____
  _____
  _____

69

NOTES: _____

_____

_____

_____

_____

_____

_____

_____

_____

_____

_____

_____

_____

_____

_____

_____

_____

_____

- Am I able to "walk in" to be seen OR do I need to make an appointment? _____

  _____

- What is the phone number of the Health Center? _____

- What are the hours of operation? Weekdays_____

  Weekends _____

- Who staffs the Health Center? _____

  _____

- Is there always a medical doctor at the clinic or is he or she available only on certain
  days?_____

- What are his or her qualifications or specialty? _____

  _____

- Is there always a registered nurse at the Health Center? _____

  _____

- When do I go to the Health Center? Just for very serious conditions, or also for
  aches, or pains, or simply when I'm not feeling up to par, etc.? _____

  _____

- Does the Center provide regular vaccinations, like for the flu? _____

- If I have a medical emergency, is there a 24-hour number I can call to determine
  whether to go to the Health Center or the nearest Emergency Room? _____

  _____

- What is the name of the nearest hospital/emergency room and what is the phone
  number? How far away from campus is it?_____

  _____

- Am I charged for every visit to the Health Center? _____

- Is there a standard fee to be seen in the Health Center? If so, what is it? _____

  _____

- Is health insurance accepted for payment? _____

- If yes, is my carrier (give them your plan's name) on the accepted list? _____

  _____

- (If the answers are "yes" to the insurance questions above): Does the health center
  file the claim for service for me or do I have to get my parents to file it for me? _____

  _____

  _____

NOTES: _____

Prescriptions for medication

- Will the Health Center fill any prescriptions it writes for me? _____
  _____

- If yes, can my personal physician also call the Health Center to fill prescriptions for me? _____
  _____

- If not at the Health Center, where do I go to have my prescriptions filled? _____
  _____

- If I take medication regularly, can the Health Center, after receiving my doctor's orders for this medication, write prescriptions for refills, or does my own doctor have to continue to write my prescriptions for me? _____
  _____

- If not, can my own doctor call in prescriptions for me to a local pharmacy? _____
  _____

- Or do I have to have my prescriptions filled at home and mailed to me?_____
  _____

- What is the best pharmacy close to campus you can recommend? How far is it? ___
  _____

Medical Records

- Prior to arriving on campus, am I required to have a physical exam, or specific immunizations? If so, to what address and to whose attention do I send the results of my physical and my immunization record? _____
  _____

- Is there any reason why I would need to send a copy of my medical records to the Health Center prior to my arrival on campus? _____
  _____

- Before I arrive on campus, am I required to receive specific immunizations? If so, which ones? _____
  _____

Glasses/Contacts

- Is there an ophthalmologist close by you can refer me to? _____
  _____

- Is there an optician you can refer me to? _____
  _____

NOTES: _____

_____

_____

_____

_____

_____

_____

_____

_____

_____

_____

_____

_____

_____

_____

_____

_____

_____

Mental Health

- Does the Health Center offer mental health services and or counseling resources? _____

- If yes, please describe what's available. _____
_____

- How do I access the help if it's needed? _____
_____

- How are these services charged? _____
_____

COMPLETE: _____

Are you feeling smart? You're getting lots of thorough information – and at a pretty quick pace, right? But don't get too smug yet; the tour has still got places to go and resources to uncover. Next...

✳✳✳✳✳✳✳

THE I.T. DEPARTMENT

Information Technology: Each college has its own way of handling the technology that will run your child's life as a student. The I.T. department is responsible for all information pertinent to the technological space.

If you are visiting campus, you might want to go to the department directly and ask to speak with one of the tech advisors – they possess an incredible amount of useful information, and can explain in simple English what action your child needs to take in order to be plugged in and turned on in all the right ways. If you are on campus, be sure your child has a computer on hand. They will probably be able to get their computer configured well in advance of Move-In Day, and this makes for a much smoother transition.

If your child is phone shopping for advice, make sure that he or she has a computer handy. The tech advisor will undoubtedly be able to help download at least some of the necessary information and programs, and help establish campus email access.

It's ideal that your child gets plugged into the college's computer system NOW. All of his or her incoming classmates will need to get their computers configured correctly when they arrive on campus, Therefore, if you wait to get this done until Move-In Day, there will be a backlog, and it could be several days before your child is able to use the college computer network. So it's important, if at all possible, to get done now whatever you can to ensure that your child is on the college's information highway from the get-go.

NOTES: _____

_____

_____

_____

_____

_____

_____

_____

_____

_____

_____

_____

_____

_____

_____

_____

_____

_____

_____

_____

Have your son or daughter ask the I.T. contact:

- What specific programs do I need to have on my computer to be compatible with the college's requirements? _____
_____

- Can you load them on my computer for me now (if visiting) or (if on the phone) can I download what I need from where I am? _____
_____

- How do I get a campus e-mail address? _____
_____

- Can you set up an email address for me now? _____
_____

- Is there WI-FI campus-wide? _____
- If not, where is it available? _____
_____

- Where are printers located for student use, and are they free? _____
_____

- What kind of ongoing tech support is available to me? _____
_____
_____

- When I have problems with my computer, is there someone I can go to for help?___
_____

- Is there a tech support person located in each dorm? _____
_____

- Are there special computer offers for students through the IT Department or through the Book Store? _____
TIP: Almost every college has some new-computer-buying plan, so be sure to do your research. _____
_____

COMPLETE:_____

Moving on, a next important "must see" on your tour is the Bookstore.

✱✱✱✱✱✱✱

NOTES: _____

_____

_____

_____

_____

_____

_____

_____

_____

_____

_____

_____

_____

_____

_____

_____

_____

_____

THE CAMPUS BOOKSTORE

A major hub of campus life is the Bookstore, or Co-op as it is sometimes known. Whether in person or by phone, your child should ask to talk to someone who can speak knowledgeably about the book-buying process for courses. If speaking by phone, it will be helpful to simultaneously reference the bookstore website.

While the Bookstore is usually full of fun items, such as logo-ed clothing, mugs and desk supplies (with more things festooned by your school's name than you ever might have imagined), your visit now is about the course books that you'll be using...

Book Buying

- What is the actual process for getting course books? Can I pre-order my books or do I purchase them in person when I arrive on campus? _____

  _____

- If the Bookstore tracks my schedule and holds the books I need, when can I pick them up? _____
- Are there designated days for freshman book buying?_____

  _____

Computer "deals" at the Bookstore

- Most campus bookstores offer special student deals on computer stuff. What are they? _____

- How do I go about purchasing a computer or other related hardware items? _____

  _____

  _____

What else does the Bookstore offer?
   TIP: Check out the store's website.

- Is a full range of school supplies available? _____
- Are items for my dorm available, (e.g. for storage, general use, cool stuff?) _____

  _____

- Are basic food items for sale? _____

  _____

NOTES: _____

_____

_____

_____

_____

_____

_____

_____

_____

_____

_____

_____

_____

_____

_____

_____

_____

_____

_____

- Are basic toiletries for sale? _____
- Are gift items available? _____

∗∗∗∗∗∗∗

SPECIAL RESOURCES

All colleges have a department dedicated to assisting students who have special learning needs, though its name will differ from school to school. Your child may need extra time on tests and exams, require a certain type of housing, or any of a long list of special needs. If your child fits in this category, ask the Switchboard Operator, or call the Freshman Dean's office or the Admissions Office to find out the exact name. Then, if this is something you're child will be needing, do your thing – contact the department, in person or on the phone, and find out just what they can do for your child. Do not miss this department; it's dedicated to making sure your son or daughter makes it in college. Their help will be invaluable. Here's what your child should ask:

- What is the exact name of the department? _____
  _____
- How is this department organized? _____
  _____
- When and who do I need to contact in this department if I feel I have a special need? _____
  _____
- Is a personally scheduled, one-on-one meeting required to access the available resources? _____
  _____
- If yes, with whom do I schedule the meeting? _____
  _____
- Will I need to provide medical information diagnosing my particular need? _____
  _____
- What special information will I have to provide? _____
  _____
- When should I get this information to the Department? _____
  _____

NOTES: _____

_____

_____

_____

_____

_____

_____

_____

_____

_____

_____

_____

_____

_____

_____

_____

_____

_____

_____

_____

_____

- Is it to be sent to the Department (and if so, to whom, exactly) prior to my arrival on campus? _____
- What are the specific resources/services provided? _____
  _____
  _____
- Will I get help in selecting courses and professors? _____
- Is help readily and easily accessible? _____
  _____
- Is there a designated center or building where studying can be done? _____
  _____
- Are tutors available through this department? _____
  _____
- If yes, are the tutors provided as a free service or is there a fee charged for their time? _____
- If there is a fee, what is it (hourly, etc.)? _____
  _____
- If tutors are not provided through this department, how do I find one, in case one is needed? _____
  _____
  _____
  _____

COMPLETE:_____

＊＊＊＊＊＊＊

THE ATHLETIC DEPARTMENT

These students know who they are — they are the ones who will be wearing their college's school colors while doing battle on the court or playing field. They no doubt have been told and re-told what is expected of them when they enter their college's gates as Freshmen. But, just in case your student athlete has NOT been told, now is the time to ask. See Chapter 5 for specific information you both need to know.

COMPLETE:_____

NOTES: _____

_____

_____

_____

_____

_____

_____

_____

_____

_____

_____

_____

_____

_____

_____

_____

_____

_____

_____

CHAPTER 4

DATA GATHERING - THE COMMUNITY

Not having the information you need when you need it leaves you wanting.
Not knowing where to look for that information leaves you powerless.
In a society where information is king, none of us can afford that.
Lois Horowitz

You and your child have made lists with questions you did not even know needed to be asked, and you have now trekked and talked yourself around the new soon-to-be college home. You must be feeling pretty confident about the transition in front of you. But don't put this manual away quite yet. There is more that you need to learn before you pronounce yourself DONE with data gathering. Just hang in with us, and ask a few more questions.

This time, the subject is the surrounding community (whether it's a tiny town or a large city) that your child will soon call home. You would never make a move from one town to another without asking these questions, and moving is just what your child is doing. He or she is leaving familiar terrain for foreign territory. They now know what's required to create a smooth transition and be able to enjoy, not puzzle over, their new environment on campus. They simply need to gather information about what awaits in the broader environment! Here is what they need to know:

GETTING THERE

What a nonsensically obvious topic this is, right? Wrong! If you haven't yet visited your college, review the directions provided on its website or brochure. If you live far enough away that flying to school is your best option, you will find that most college websites have helpful information about which airport(s) to use, and provide clear driving directions from the airport to school. In any case, you and your child would be wise to (here we go again) do a bit of research:

NOTES: _____

_____

_____

_____

_____

_____

_____

_____

_____

_____

_____

_____

_____

_____

_____

_____

_____

_____

Air Travel

- Which airport(s) is/are in the vicinity of your school? _____
  _____

- What airlines fly into it/them? _____
  _____
  _____

- What flights are there, direct or indirect? TIP: Sometimes indirect flights are cheaper because they fly through "hub" cities and may provide more choices and price options. _____
  _____
  _____
  _____

- Look at your academic calendar to see when holidays and other breaks begin and end. Put those dates on your calendar, and then be pro-active and book your flights EARLY, as rates soar and capacity is limited around peak seasons.
  _____

Transportation to and from airport to college

- Are there buses or other mass transportation available? _____
  _____

- If you are in a remote location where transportation is difficult, are there special transportation options provided by your college available during peak college holiday times?_____
  _____

- How are you able to get information about your options? Note: You may want to ask someone in Residential Life about this._____
  _____

COMPLETE:_____

SETTING UP YOUR NEW LIFE

As we have said before, a move to college is more than just changing where sleep takes place! Your child's whole life in all its routines will be impacted because he or she IS MOVING...in all ways. So, to get off to a quick and pleasant start, your student would be wise to get familiar with the basic services that will be needed in the new community. The

NOTES: _____

_____

_____

_____

_____

_____

_____

_____

_____

_____

_____

_____

_____

_____

_____

_____

_____

sooner you find out where things are, the better. And this is most important with basic services and those elements of the new community that your child may want to access right away.

As we mentioned earlier: You should ask your list of contacts about the services that are close to your college and known to be "student friendly." You may already have obtained some of this information from the Residential Life staff. But there are several categories to make sure about. First, we'll start with a topic that's of keen interest to any young person living away from the family for the first time in any extended way: money.

BANKING

TIP: There is no need to explain how important this aspect is going to be for you. Access to money is like access to food and medical services. It's important to know where to go for cash, and for help with other money matters, and it's good to know it soon.

First, if your child is going off to school in the same state, your family bank may have a branch in the college's town. If you deal with a regional or national bank, they may also have a branch even in the most remote out-of-state locations. So here are the questions for your student to explore.

Your current bank -

• Is there a local branch in my new town? Where? _____
_____

TIP: If yes, then if you have a personal account already, you might consider changing branches, and making personal introductions with some of the staff at the new location, since this can make everything go more smoothly. The best time to meet bank folks is not when you have a problem, but when you're arriving as a new customer.

• Does my bank have an ATM convenient to the school?_____
_____

• Can my ATM card be used in the machines around campus?_____
_____

A local bank -

• If my bank is not represented in my college town, what is a student-friendly bank?
_____

• Where is the closest branch to campus? _____
_____

• Is there someone specifically designated to handle student accounts? _____
_____

NOTES: _____

_____

_____

_____

_____

_____

_____

_____

_____

_____

_____

_____

_____

_____

_____

_____

_____

_____

_____

- Are there ATM's convenient to campus? _____
_____

- Is there one actually on campus? _____
_____

- Are there any special student banking plans? _____
_____
_____

PHARMACY

If you have found out in your Health Center conversation that you will need to get prescriptions filled off-campus, you will of course need a pharmacy.

- Is there a reliable, student-friendly pharmacy close to campus that delivers? TIP: Ask the Health Center for a recommendation. _____
_____

- Does it honor my insurance? _____
_____

- Does the pharmacy have charge accounts? _____
_____

- If yes, how can I open one? _____
_____
_____

COMPLETE:_____

FOOD SHOPPING

It's truer in college than at any other time...food makes the world go 'round! This is why many dining halls or food facilities are open all hours of the night. That's also why there are microwaves and small refrigerators in almost all rooms. In some dorms with suites or common rooms, there may also be stoves, ovens, larger refrigerators and microwaves, etc.

You are more nocturnal than ever in college, and there is nothing like late night food to keep you going. And of course, if you are up late at night, you may not want to get up early to get to the dining hall before class. What's the solution? Groceries in your room! You'll want to keep on hand stuff like milk, cereal, bread, peanut butter, jam, soup, bottled water, soft drinks, sports drinks, fruit, paper goods and plastic ware. To keep the room stocked,

NOTES: _____

_____

_____

_____

_____

_____

_____

_____

_____

_____

_____

_____

_____

_____

_____

_____

_____

_____

you'll need to know where to shop. This information should be available from the Residential Life team.

- Where is the closest convenience store to campus? _____
_____
- What are its hours? _____
_____
- For more serious grocery shopping, where do I go? _____
_____
_____

COMPLETE:_____

RESTAURANTS

Food makes the world go 'round outside the dorm room, too! Be curious and have fun with your search for great food. Here is what you will want to be sure to know:

- What are the best restaurants in the area? _____
_____
- Where is the best place for breakfast? _____
_____
- Who serves a great hamburger? _____
_____
- What is the favorite late-night spot? _____
_____
- Any great ethnic restaurants? _____
_____
- Where is the best coffee house or Starbucks? _____
_____
- Can I make a reservation at any of these places? _____
_____

COMPLETE:_____

KEEPING FAITH ALIVE

If faith is important in your child's life, we cannot stress enough how important it is for you to know where the closest church, synagogue, or other religious house of worship is located.

NOTES: _____

_____

_____

_____

_____

_____

_____

_____

_____

_____

_____

_____

_____

_____

_____

_____

_____

_____

Even though most colleges have on-campus religious communities, the time may come when your child seeks a private place away from campus to nourish their soul and mind. Such a place allows them to go beyond their role as a student and become a part of a special community. They may foster meaningful relationships with a pastor, priest, or rabbi who can be an oasis away from the maelstrom of campus life.

Search online for your denomination's locations close to campus. Call and speak to the person in charge of new members, and before making a choice, be sure your child visits each one to determine the best fit.

Consider asking:

- How close is each place of worship to campus? _____
  _____

- Do they cater to the campus student population?_____
  _____

- Is there a person responsible for college outreach? If so, what is his/her name and contact information? _____
  _____

- When are services held? _____
  _____

- How large is the congregation?_____
  _____

COMPLETE:_____

POST OFFICE/MAILING FACILITIES

If the campus mail center does not provide specialized mailing services, you will need to ask these questions:

- Where is the nearest U. S. Post Office? _____
  _____

- Where is the closest UPS pickup and delivery? _____
  _____

- Where can I drop off a FedEx package? _____
  _____

- Are there other options? _____ If yes, where? _____
  _____

- Will the facility hold packages for me prior to my arrival for Freshman Move-In? __
  _____

COMPLETE:_____

NOTES: _____

_____

_____

_____

_____

_____

_____

_____

_____

_____

_____

_____

_____

_____

_____

_____

_____

_____

STORAGE OPTIONS

As we mentioned previously, if you live beyond an easy driving distance of your college, or if you just have a lot of stuff, you will need to find a storage facility to store possessions between school terms. This may even be an attractive option for those who live within driving distance, but do not want to clutter their homes with college furniture and mementos. After seeing the size of the dorm room, you may decide that you could use extra space to store out-of-season clothes/shoes, and may want to secure a storage space for the entire year. Consider sharing a space with another family to defray your costs.

TIP: Summer time presents a big issue, as it is impractical to bring anything except your clothes back home at the end of the school year. There are a few web-based college storage companies who will provide boxes, pick up your child's items at their room on a designated date and then redeliver them when they return in the fall. You may want to ask the campus residential life people what students ordinarily do about storage.

Here are some points to inquire about:

PERSONAL STORAGE UNITS

- What types of storage facilities are available? _____
  _____
  _____

- Are there storage facilities close to campus? _____
  _____

- What are their names? _____
  _____

- Is it difficult to secure a storage space and if yes, how far in advance should I contract for one? _____
  _____
  _____

ALTERNATIVE STORAGE SOLUTIONS

- Are there other storage solutions? If so, what are they? _____
  _____

- Is there a web-based storage company that services this campus (such as CollegeBoxes.com)? _____
  _____

COMPLETE:_____

97

NOTES: _____

_____

_____

_____

_____

_____

_____

_____

_____

_____

_____

_____

_____

_____

_____

_____

_____

_____

DON'T LEAVE HOME WITHOUT IT

Information from the home crowd that connects with your new life, that is! Don't be shy! Here are the people you need to be in touch with:

- ❖ Incoming students who live in your area
- ❖ Current students who live in your area
- ❖ Alums who live in your area

These people can be tremendous resources for information and helpful tips about your new environment, but only if you have a way to get in touch with them!

Admissions officers can be a valuable source of information about local student and alumni communities. Call and ask for the names and contact information of people in all three groups, including the name of at least one active alumnus or alumna in your area.

With the names of local students and alumni in-hand, your child can use social networking websites to retrieve more information about them, determine who may be of special interest, and initiate conversations with those individuals. Perhaps they can meet for a cup of coffee to discuss how things *really* work at the college. Your son or daughter has a lot to gain – he or she will make new friends, absorb countless useful tidbits, and upon arriving on campus, will have the comfort of having insider information and even of seeing a familiar face.

When speaking with local alumni, your child should ask these questions:

- Is there an active alumni club in my town? _____
  _____

- Can you plug me into the group or is there someone else I should talk to (get name and contact info)? _____
  _____

- Are there any summer functions for new students and alumni? _____
  _____
  _____

- Is there a summer send-off party? If so, when and where? _____
  _____
  _____

COMPLETE:_____

NOTES: _____

_____

_____

_____

_____

_____

_____

_____

_____

_____

_____

_____

_____

_____

_____

_____

_____

_____

HOTELS, INNS, B&B'S

For Parents: So far, we have been digging for all sorts of data to help the incoming freshman. But the following information is exclusively for you, the parents. After all, when you are planning, moving, and hauling, you will want a comfortable place to rest your head. All schools list hotels on their website under "Visitors." But just because a place is listed, that doesn't mean you would want to stay there. So what do you do? You know the answer...you ASK! If you are going into a large college community, the choices will be ample and securing room reservations will pose no problem. If, however, your new college is in a small town or remote area, you may be really challenged to find visitor accommodations. This is a subject that merits asking lots of questions. Here is what to ask:

Finding a Place to Stay:

- What types of accommodations are available? _____
  _____

- What are the best (or best value) nearby hotels? _____
  _____
  _____

- Are there nice motels or budget hotels nearby? _____
  _____

- Are there bed and breakfast inns convenient to the campus? _____
  _____

- Where do most visitors tend to stay for visits or Move In Day?_____
  _____

- How far in advance must reservations be made to get your place of choice for parents' weekend and football weekends? _____
  _____

  - Are there special discounts for college visitors? _____
    _____

In some remote college locations, residents in the community rent out their houses for big college weekends. If this applies to you, ask the Residential Life representatives the following:
- Are there websites featuring local homes to rent? If so, what are they? _____
  _____

- Is there a real estate agent in town with expertise in this area? _____
  _____

- How soon must reservations be made for important campus events? _____
  _____

COMPLETE:_____

NOTES: _____

_____

_____

_____

_____

_____

_____

_____

_____

_____

_____

_____

_____

_____

_____

_____

_____

_____

These are all questions we've found it useful to ask. Gathering the relevant data will put knowledge and power into your hands for a successful move. Remember, the unknown can unhinge us – the known we can deal with. And it's always better to have more information than you need than to lack that one crucial answer that could have made all the difference! The more preparation that you and your child do now, the smoother and more successful the coming move will be.

NOTES: _____

_____

_____

_____

_____

_____

_____

_____

_____

_____

_____

_____

_____

_____

_____

_____

_____

CHAPTER 5

RECRUITED ATHLETES

We may all come on different ships,
but we are in the same boat.
Martin Luther King Jr.

If your child is entering college as a recruited athlete, congratulations! He or she is a member of an elite group of highly motivated young men and women whose college experience will be significantly formed by their sports experience.

But with the glory comes the reality of an earlier move-in date than regular incoming freshmen. This means you have to be on top of your college-preparation game sooner than the rest.

Your child has undoubtedly received from their coach and the Athletic Department plenty of information about what is expected of them athletically upon entering the college's gates – including physical conditioning and pre-season workout requirements. However, you have probably received lots of general, but precious little detailed information about your child's transition from high school star to college athlete. Even with this informational gap, your child will be expected to hit the ground running. Therefore, you would be wise to seek out answers preemptively, before your student athlete is overly consumed with the pre-season.

It is usually true that college athletes are treated differently than the general student population. They have more demanding schedules from Day One and most schools will offer support commensurate with those demands. Student athletes often have different housing assignments, different meal plans, and access to unique class schedules and services. The Athletic Department often cannot and will not provide all this information up front for you, but will likely be impressed by your child's organization and initiative when they approach the Department with questions.

In addition to the information in the preceding chapters, here are some specifics you will need to know:

NOTES: _____

_____

_____

_____

_____

_____

_____

_____

_____

_____

_____

_____

_____

_____

_____

_____

_____

_____

_____

VITAL DATES

- What date am I able to move into my room? _____
- How long do I have to get moved in? _____
- If I need to provide special medical information, what is it and when is it due?
  _____
- When will I receive any required medical forms? _____
- When are they due, and to whom do I send them? _____
  _____
- When is my first practice? How early should I arrive? _____
  _____

HOUSING INFORMATION

- Am I in an all-athlete dorm (if applicable)? _____
  _____
- What is the name of the dorm? _____
  _____
- Can I choose my own roommate or is he/she assigned? _____
  _____
- Am I able to express my preferences? _____
  _____
- Has my roommate already been assigned/? _____
  _____
- If yes, who is it and what is the contact info? _____
  _____
- If no, when will I know who my roommate is? _____
  _____
- If my dorm is a designated athlete dorm, is it different than the other dorm
  rooms in regular student housing? _____
  _____
- If yes, what are the differences? _____
  _____
- What are the items provided in the room? _____
  _____
  _____

NOTES: _____

_____

_____

_____

_____

_____

_____

_____

_____

_____

_____

_____

_____

_____

_____

_____

_____

_____

SERVICES PROVIDED FOR ATHLETES

- Is there an athlete-only cafeteria? _____
- If yes, can I also use other campus "eateries"? _____
  _____

- If you are on a partial scholarship, is there a special "athlete only" meal plan?
  _____

- Is general laundry service provided or does it only apply to uniforms/athletic clothing only? _____
  _____

- What clothing will I be provided (so you will know what you need to buy or pack)? _____
  _____

- Is special counseling available to me if I need it? _____
  _____

ACADEMIC SUPPORT

- Is there someone to advise me on determining my schedule? _____
  _____

- Who is it and I how and when can I have contact with him/her? _____
  _____

- Is there a special athletic study center? _____
  _____

- Are specific study hours required?_____
  _____

- Are subject tutors available? If so, how do I get in touch with them? _____
  _____

COMPLETE:_____

******

The Athlete and the Broader Community

If your child is going to be attending college as a recruited athlete, one more thing is important to remember. It's good to have a diversity of friends in life. It will be natural for your child to associate mainly with fellow teammates, or even with recruited athletes in other

NOTES: _____

_____

_____

_____

_____

_____

_____

_____

_____

_____

_____

_____

_____

_____

_____

_____

_____

sports. They will all face common pressures, and similar challenges. They may be living and eating in close proximity with each other, and it's normal for young people to hang out with people with whom they have a lot in common. But it's important for them to remember they have a lot in common with non-athletes at the new school as well.

You've all been through a rigorous and demanding process of application and selection. The school has sought to bring to campus the best mix of young people possible for the making of a great overall community. Your child may find friendships outside of their sport, or outside of athletics altogether, that will be among the best and most important friendships they'll ever have for life. Because of this, and to give it a better chance of happening, your child's preparation for moving to campus should not just involve a laser-like focus on the athletic side of things. The more other students and non-athletic alumni they get to know, the better. There is a whole world of excellent experiences to be had at college, and an open mind toward meeting and befriending other students outside the team can enhance those experiences immeasurably.

NOTES: _____

_____

_____

_____

_____

_____

_____

_____

_____

_____

_____

_____

_____

_____

_____

_____

_____

_____

CHAPTER 6
THE DORM ROOM AND ROOMATE

Prepare and prevent; don't repair and repent.
Author unknown

The dorm is, quite simply, the base of operations, the retreat, and the nerve center. It is the soft place to fall, the office, the entertaining spot, and the inner sanctum. This is why approaching the dorm room as more than a room with a bed and a desk is so integral to a great college experience.

A dorm room is as unique as *your child's* personality. Some students will want it to be cute, some will want it to be sparse, but each needs it to be functional. This is one area of college life that you really need to get right, because as the dorm room goes, so goes one's feeling of home AND productivity as a student.

This chapter is accordingly dedicated to helping you understand the challenges that face you in creating a space that will be essential to your child's comfort and productivity (not to mention sanity!). We'll help you formulate and execute a plan that will be functional, but will also reflect your child's personal style.

Dorms, by definition, are small, cramped spaces that will test your powers of creative planning. When we say small, we mean small. Even at their best, with two roommates for whom organization and tidiness are a priority, dorms rooms are inevitably islands of clutter. If you add to the mix a roommate whose personality thrives in disorder, your mind can only wander as to how difficult the living situation can be.

Because the dorm room is SO important, we have placed great emphasis in this book on the physical attributes of the room, and have provided a shopping list replete with ideas for products that can multitask or enable you to utilize hard-to-use or easily forgotten spaces.

You cannot change the physical layout of the room, as much as you might be tempted by dreams of sledgehammers and carpentry crews. Fortunately, there is a wide range of creative products in the marketplace designed with dorm rooms in mind. These products will enable you to organize the chaos that is typical of a dorm room to the extent that you choose.

NOTES: _____

_____

_____

_____

_____

_____

_____

_____

_____

_____

_____

_____

_____

_____

_____

_____

_____

Keep in mind as you shop for your child's new room that the items you buy should be portable, compact, often able to solve more than one "problem," and they should especially be durable. Durability is important because whatever you move in will have to be moved out, and back – again and again.

Also worth consideration is the psychological change your child will undergo in transitioning from their own room at home to a room shared with a new person. The change will be striking, even if your son or daughter is planning to live with someone they already know. It's a new level of enforced sociability and will go best if each party approaches the situation with a determination to exhibit optimism, friendliness, and kindness in all things. Roommates don't have to become best friends, but things are always smoother and more enjoyable if they're both understanding and friendly.

Before selecting a roommate, your child needs to consider his or her own needs and desires. When they receive roommate preference forms, make sure they take time to do an honest personal appraisal – the good, the bad and the ugly about themselves, as well as the kind of roommate THEY think they will be. This is an important time for candid self-examination and open expression. Then, they should include information on the form (even an extra page, if necessary) about the attributes they seek in a roommate. This will allow the college staff charged with matching roommates to "hear" your child's voice and match him or her most compatibly. There's hardly anything worse in college life than a bad roommate match and hardly anything better than a good one. The dorm room needs to be a place of emotional safety, relaxation, pleasantness, and calm. Any time and attention spent on this issue up front can pay off crucially.

The die is cast. Upon receiving their rooming assignment from the school, your child should:

- Contact the new roommate immediately.

- Get acquainted over the phone, by email, and even by video chat.

- Take a careful look at the specific floor plan of the dorm room assigned (which, hopefully, should be available on the school's website).

- Using the data gathered in Chapter 3, visualize the room and talk with the roommate about the items they think they will need (e.g. TV, refrigerator, microwave, etc). To avoid duplication, discuss who has what and/or who will provide what.

NOTES: _____

_____

_____

_____

_____

_____

_____

_____

_____

_____

_____

_____

_____

_____

_____

_____

_____

_____

- Talk about how coordinated they want their room to be.
  - Do you want to use a color scheme?
  - Do you want to have matching comforters, etc.?

- Talk about how they might want to configure the room, (e.g. bunk beds, raised beds so that you can put a sofa or desks underneath to free up floor space). This discussion will help generate a list of furniture for purchase.

- If your child finds his or her new roommate to be compatible and the two decide to work in concert on decorating the room, they should discuss the idea of meeting at school a couple of days before Freshman Move-In to do some shopping together.

- Coordinate purchases by using the same websites and shopping on-line.

Even randomly assigned roommates can end up being friends for life. Remember, the college has worked hard to admit only people its admissions staff believe to be great potential members of the community. They've typically sorted out an extraordinary group of students. If you communicate your needs and desires, then work to get to know your assigned roommate; chances are that you'll have a great year together.

NOTES: _____

_____

_____

_____

_____

_____

_____

_____

_____

_____

_____

_____

_____

_____

_____

_____

_____

_____

CHAPTER 7

LISTS AND SHOPPING FOR THE ROOM

Don't agonize...organize!
Florynce Kennith

If your student and new roommate have talked, you may already have an idea of what they want their room to look like and how they want it to function. Even if they haven't yet had that conversation, you probably already have some at least preliminary thoughts about it. Through data gathering, you already better understand the college campus and the resources available in the greater community. It's now time to work on finalizing a Master List of what your child needs for college. Remember, space is limited and creativity is king. You want to take advantage of every bit of space that's available for you. And to do this, you absolutely must think vertically — use those walls!

Before you focus too much on the shopping lists, visit the college's website and see if you can find room layouts and dimensions for the unit your child has been assigned. This will help you experiment with furniture layout, maximize space and prevent you from over-buying. And when you see those dimensions, take a deep breath. Monks live in small spaces. And astronauts. Generations of students before have managed just fine with the square footage available, and your student will, too!

We have included at the end of this chapter an exhaustive shopping list. But first, let us issue a word of caution — it is overwhelming, but includes a sampling of everything you could possibly purchase and send to college. We expect that upon reading our list, you'll cut it down to what you feel is necessary and relevant to your child.

Here are things to consider as you finalize your personal list:

- Always think about using items that can serve multiple purposes

    - Stacking shelves can double as a nightstand or printer stand.
    - Hanging shelf bags can hold not just shoes and sweaters, but any comparably light items in need of storage.

NOTES: _____

_____

_____

_____

_____

_____

_____

_____

_____

_____

_____

_____

_____

_____

_____

_____

_____

_____

- Utilize the space on university-provided items

  - Desks with hutches – find decorative boxes to place on the shelves to expand storage; they are functional and also add color and style to the room.
  - Hang a mirror on one side of the wardrobe door. Put stacking wire shelves in the wardrobe/closet for shoe storage. Use stacking shelves on top of the wardrobe as additional storage space. House TV or electronic equipment on top of the dresser.

- If the bed lofts, that will provide a significant amount of extra space, so plan to use every cubic inch of it to your benefit.

  - Maximize the utility of the under-bed space by purchasing a stacking drawer unit.
  - Fill the rest of the space with a duffle bag, plastic storage boxes (see below), and other items that you want out of the way.

- If the bed bunks, then the under-bed space will be shared with your child's roommate, requiring super-efficiency on your part.

- Clear storage boxes enable you to easily store/stack under the bed, on shelves, etc. They come in many sizes, and you will want plenty!

  - Oversized under-bed boxes are perfect for holding extra sheets, towels, and a blanket.
  - Regular size under-bed boxes are ideal catch-alls for extra school supplies, extra toiletries, cleaning supplies, out of season clothing, etc.
  - Shoebox sizes are perfect for holding smaller items or for organizing drawers in your child's dresser.
  - Small plastic boxes work well as drawer organizers for the desk and hutch.

- A stacking drawer unit is one of the most multi-purpose items you can buy. Try to be creative and use them wherever you can. They will give you much-needed valuable extra space, both in the drawers and on top.

  - Use a stacking drawer unit as a bedside table.
  - Use one as a stand for your printer.

NOTES: _____

_____

_____

_____

_____

_____

_____

_____

_____

_____

_____

_____

_____

_____

_____

_____

_____

- The top can be a platform for your microwave or mini-fridge (some have a sturdy, thick top that can support those sorts of things).
- Drawers can be used for computer supplies, kitchen items, food, paper towels, etc. – depending on how you're using them.

- Do not overlook wall and vertical space – even if you are forbidden from nailing anything to the walls, you can still use them!

- Use adhesive utility hooks (such as 3-M brand Command Hooks), which, depending on their size, can even hold wire shelves. They are perfect for holding towels, bathrobes, coats, etc.

- Consider folding bookshelves. They can hold much more than books.

- If no shelves are provided, consider plastic crates and cubes as bookshelves and catch-alls. They stack on top of each other, providing significant storage, while taking up a minimal amount of space. They even come in many colors, serving an aesthetic purpose.

Before you head off shopping, consider what you would like to send to college. Peruse the lists at the end of this chapter, which are designed to make your child's room efficient and their college life organized. Approach purchases with the mantra of "A place for everything, and everything in its place." This is a good time to take out the mental scalpel and cut out non-essential items.

The following list of stores will guide you to places that are loaded with dorm-friendly items, whether you shop in-person or online. When shopping, remember to bring not only a to-do list, but also a desire for a second opinion. Seek out the most experienced salesperson and pick his or her brain. They can provide you with a wealth of information on which products work best in a dorm room setting.

Some retailers, like Bed, Bath & Beyond, offer a very special service. You can shop in your local store, pick out what you want, buy it, and pick it up at the store of theirs closest to your campus. Ask about this service if it would be helpful to you!

NOTES: _____

_____

_____

_____

_____

_____

_____

_____

_____

_____

_____

_____

_____

_____

_____

_____

_____

_____

COLLEGE-FRIENDLY RETAILERS

Bed, Bath & Beyond
Best Buy
Big Lots
BJ's Discount Club
Costco

Container Store
Ikea
J C Penny
K-Mart
Office Depot

Office Max
Sam's
Staples
Target
Wal-Mart

COLLEGE-FRIENDLY RETAIL WEBSITES

Amazon.com
ContainerStore.com
DormBuys.com

Overstock.com
PBTeen.com
Levenger.com

NOTES: _____

_____

_____

_____

_____

_____

_____

_____

_____

_____

_____

_____

_____

_____

_____

_____

_____

_____

SHOPPING LIST

	Got it?	Buy it/Where	Pack it	Ship it
BED & BEDDING				
Bedspread/comforter				
Sheet sets (2+) - twin XL				
Blanket (consider thermal)				
Throw (fleece, etc.) for foot of bed				
Mattress pad				
Feather bed/foam egg crate pad				
Pillows for sleeping/lounging/shams				
Bed risers				
	Got it?	Buy it/Where	Pack it	Ship it
ORGANIZERS/CONTAINERS				
shoe box size				
under bed size (regular & long)				
sweater size				
misc. sizes				
Multi-drawer/stackable drawer units				
Hang3rs (plenty!)				
with clips				
without clips				
Tiered				
Wire stacking shelves				
Over-the-door shoe hanger				
Folding shelf unit				
Plastic crates/cubes				
Plastic hooks - multi sizes (3M Command)				
Vacuum storage bags				
Belt hanger				
Underbed drawers				
Stacking mesh shelves				
Wall grid system & accessories				
Over the door hooks (various)				
Multi-tiered cart on wheels				
Large, thin trash can				
Drawer dividers				

NOTES:_____

_____

_____

_____

_____

_____

_____

_____

_____

_____

_____

_____

_____

_____

_____

_____

_____

_____

_____

_____

	Got it?	Buy it/Where	Pack it	Ship it
DESK				
Drawer organizers - various sizes				
Desk lamp - clip-on or desktop				
Book ends				
Basic desk/school supplies				
Desk chair (optional)				
Printer ink and cables				
White board/eraser/markers				
Bulletin board/memory board & push pins				
Clock radio				
Telephone (if land line required)				
	Got it?	Buy it/Where	Pack it	Ship it
BATH				
Bath robe				
Towels (2+ sets) - bath, hand, wash				
Shower caddy/tote				
Shower shoes/flip flops				
	Got it?	Buy it/Where	Pack it	Ship it
TOILETRIES/MEDICINES				
First aid supplies				
Bath products				
Personal grooming products				
OTC medicines				
Sunscreen				
Prescription meds				
Basic toiletries				
First aid supplies				
	Got it?	Buy it/Where	Pack it	Ship it
LAUNDRY				
Laundry bags (2) or Hamper				
Detergent & fabric softener				
Lint roller				
Spray stain remover				
Bleach				
Iron				
Mini ironing board (or folding)				

NOTES:_____

_____

_____

_____

_____

_____

_____

_____

_____

_____

_____

_____

_____

_____

_____

_____

_____

_____

_____

_____

Plastic tote w/ handles to hold laundry supplies				

	Got it?	Buy it/Where	Pack it	Ship it
IN ROOM KITCHEN				
Mini frig (know cubic footage allowed)				
Microwave (know wattage allowed)				
Sandwich maker/grill				
Toaster oven				
Small coffee maker				
Electric kettle				
Blender				
Bowls, plates, mugs, cups				
Plastic or stainless cutlery				
Bottle opener				
Can opener				
Paper napkins				
Paper towels & holder				
Canisters/snap-ware				
Chip clips				
Zip lock bags				
Hot pads				
Dish soap, rags/sponges, towels				
Plastic wrap/aluminum foil				
	Got it?	Buy it/Where	Pack it	Ship it
CLEANING				
Windex/surface cleaner				
Stick vac/compact carpet sweeper				
Small cordless vac				
Plastic trash can & liners				
Air freshener				
Dust pan set				
	Got it?	Buy it/Where	Pack it	Ship it
CORDS & MISC.				
Extension cords (various lengths)				
Power strips/surge protector				
Ethernet cords - extra long				
USB cords - extra long				

NOTES: _____

_____

_____

_____

_____

_____

_____

_____

_____

_____

_____

_____

_____

_____

_____

_____

_____

_____

Cord identifiers/ties/wrappers			
Printer cords			
Camera cord or dock			
Cable TV cord - extra long			
Electric outlet extender plugs			
Chargers for phones/cameras/Ipod			
Laptop computer lock			

Batteries (various sizes)			
Light bulbs			
Bungie cords			
Step stool			

	Got it?	Buy it/Where	Pack it	Ship it
EXTRAS				
TV with built-in DVD player				
TV turntable				
Full length mirror				
Ottoman with storage				
Fan				
Space heater				
Area rug				
Air mattress for overnight guests				
Folding guest chair				
Medium duffle bag for short trips				
Bed lamp (floor/clip-on/bedside)				
Bike lock				
Key chain for dorm key, mailbox, bike lock				
Umbrella or rain poncho				
Wall décor				
Poster putty				
Photos from home				
Sports equipment				
Sewing kit				

NOTES: _____

_____

_____

_____

_____

_____

_____

_____

_____

_____

_____

_____

_____

_____

_____

_____

_____

	Got it?	Buy it/Where	Pack it	Ship it
MOVE-IN NECESSITIES				
Tool baggie				
Allen wrench				
regular wrench				
Pliers				
small hammer				
flat & Phillips head screwdrivers				
duct tape				
Sharpies				
Scissors				
Extra large trash bags for move-in day trash				
	Got it?	Buy it/Where	Pack it	Ship it
DORM-FRIENDLY FOOD				
Soda				
Chips				
Gatorade				
Soup				
Oatmeal				
Hot Chocolate				
Peanut Butter and Jelly				
Bread				
Cookies				
Breakfast bars				
Micro Wave cookbook				
Mac 'n Cheese				
Fruit				
Popcorn				
Cereal				
Coffee, tea bags & condiments				

NOTES: _____

_____

_____

_____

_____

_____

_____

_____

_____

_____

_____

_____

_____

_____

_____

_____

_____

_____

_____

CHAPTER 8

PACKING AND SHIPPING

*A good plan is like a road map. It shows the final destination
and the best way to get there.*
H. Stanley Judd

Y{ou} have completed your data gathering, formulated your plan, made your shopping list, and shopped 'til you've dropped. Now is the time to transport these items to college. Now, you must turn your attention to packing and shipping.

This is where the plans and ideas meet reality. And, in reality, this is a dynamic, not static, process that transpires throughout the summer. Most students put off until tomorrow what needs to be done today, especially if they are not aware of the urgency. As parents, we understand that it is too easy to underestimate the time and number of steps involved in packing for college, not to mention the actual lead time it will take for shipped items to arrive at their destination.

So, once again, we encourage a well thought-out packing and shipping plan based on the data you have accumulated in this process. Here are some ideas:

- Determine your package(s)'s destination

    - The College Mail Room – From your Data Gathering in Chapter 3, you should already know if mailing packages here is an option for you. If you did not complete that section, go back to it, call the Mail Center and get answers to the questions provided.
    - If the Mail Center does not accept packages, where can they be sent?
        - The hotel/motel where you'll stay for Freshman Move-In
        - A retail mailing and shipping store
        - The house of a friend in the area, if applicable

- Choose your shipping company

NOTES: _____

_____

_____

_____

_____

_____

_____

_____

_____

_____

_____

_____

_____

_____

_____

_____

_____

■ Use a national carrier, such as FedEx, UPS, etc. and comparison shop. Each has an 800-phone number, so call customer service. Ask every conceivable question about how to get a package picked up from your front door and delivered to college. Make your decision not just on price, but also on the level of service provided. Ask:

- Do they deliver to our chosen destination in the new college town? _____
- How many days are required for shipping by ground (the cheapest method) from my home to the destination? _____ _____
- What are the methods available for shipping? Overnight?_____ 2nd day? _____ Other?_____
- What is the process to ship a package? _____ _____ _____ _____
- Who provides the label for the package? _____ _____
- Do I need to open an account to arrange for a package pick-up? _____ _____
- If yes, how do I open the account? _____ _____
- How is shipping cost determined? _____ _____
- Is insurance available for the contents of the packages? If so, how much does it cost? _____ _____
- How are the prices for this coverage determined? _____ _____
- Am I able to track my packages online to ensure that they have arrived at my chosen destination?_____ If so, how? _____

NOTES: _____

_____

_____

_____

_____

_____

_____

_____

_____

_____

_____

_____

_____

_____

_____

_____

_____

_____

o Designate a place in your house for all items purchased or earmarked for movement to college. If possible, segregate items you are accumulating into

1. Items to be shipped
2. Things to be packed in the car (if you are driving) or
3. Items for carrying on the plane.

o Generally assess each item in terms of the most appropriate method of moving it. See more information below.

- What to do—pack or ship? Consider:

    ▪ If you are flying

        o Consider current airline guidelines that limit the size and weight of bags permitted onboard. Be sure to find out the rules laid out by your specific carrier.
        o Consider the growing frequency and incidence of lost baggage.
        o Can you realistically transport everything on the plane?
        o When these considerations are taken into account, you will quickly understand why shipping has become the "default" method of getting your goods from point A to point B.

    ▪ If you are driving

        o Is there ample room in your car for you, your family AND all of the stuff that has to go with you, or will one or two of you have to fly or drive a second car?
        o To minimize the extra hassles and expense, consider what can be shipped up-front.

- Packing—if you are flying

    ▪ Pack in the largest duffle bags possible. Side note: Do not forget to roll up and pack a medium-sized duffle to have handy for weekend trips.

    TIP: Avoid large, hard-sided suitcases unless there is space in your dorm to store them. Suitcases take up precious under-bed storage room, whereas duffle bags can be rolled up and stuffed in a far corner under the bed. They also add to the weight limits you are contending with on airplanes.

NOTES: _____

_____

_____

_____

_____

_____

_____

_____

_____

_____

_____

_____

_____

_____

_____

_____

_____

_____

- Use vacuum seal bags. They enable you to pack large quantities in what becomes a compact package after the air is sucked out with a vacuum cleaner hose. They are available in varying sizes, from retailers and online.

- Your carry-on bag for the airplane should contain several changes of clothes and toiletries for your time in the hotel, move-in day, and a couple of days beyond, in case there is any lost luggage.

- Be sure to carry-on all critical medication.

- And don't forget that laptop!

- Ship everything else, per the instructions below.

- If you cannot ship items economically, pack them in your car or carry them with you on the plane. Better yet, shop locally for them when you arrive at your college destination.

- If you plan to ship:

  - Refer to your notes pertaining to shipping via the company you have chosen as your designated shipper.

  - Schedule a pick-up for your packages, allowing for the time recommended to ensure timely delivery at your destination. Factor in a few additional days, enabling you to track and find any wayward boxes. You want them to arrive BEFORE you do.

  - Purchase medium-sized boxes for packing (to keep them from being too heavy) from moving companies, storage facilities, or online.

  - Do not over-pack your boxes, and be sure to tape them well.

  - VERY IMPORTANT: Make a separate packing list that generally describes the contents of each box you are shipping, and then number each box (1 of 5, 2 of 5, etc.). This will help you confirm that all boxes have arrived safely, with the entirety of their contents intact. On Move-In Day, you will also know what to unpack when.

NOTES: _____

_____

_____

_____

_____

_____

_____

_____

_____

_____

_____

_____

_____

_____

_____

_____

_____

_____

- TIP: <u>DO NOT LIST CONTENTS ON THE OUTSIDE OF THE PACKAGES!</u> This might seem like a natural thing to do, and it gets done all the time, but it's just far too tempting for would-be thieves and ends up being a very effective "Steal Me" sign! Keep your contexts listed on separate documents that you hold. Also keep all package shipping receipts and take them and your master list with you when you head off for Move-In Day.

  - Cut items out of rigid plastic packaging prior to shipping. This will save you some room and will also save you some time while unpacking on Move-In Day! Any little thing like this can save you crucial time on the day when you'll never have enough!

- Once the boxes are shipped off, you have time to concentrate on packing for the plane or car.

NOTES: _____

_____

_____

_____

_____

_____

_____

_____

_____

_____

_____

_____

_____

_____

_____

_____

_____

_____

CHAPTER 9

MOVE-IN DAY

In any enterprise, your perspiration will be
inversely proportional to your preparation.
Scott Sorrell

Finally, the endgame! You're on your way to Freshman Move-In! You feel prepared for the big day. You've asked and had answered more questions than you can count. You've made lists and checked them twice. You have packed and shipped boxes, and organized your car as if you were putting together a big 3-D jigsaw puzzle. Everything's going along just as you had envisioned it. After all, how difficult can it be to move a student from home to college? But wait – the REAL pitfalls are still ahead of you…

As we often say, "You don't know what you don't know." And this can be a problem! Remember those summer mailings you received from your college? What was innocuously listed as "Freshman Move-In" should have been called "TRAIN WRECK AHEAD!"

Did your packet of information tell you that it would be impossible to find a parking space? Or how the dorms either have no elevators or ones that are tediously slow and always full? Did they inform you that hallways and stairs not designed for two-way traffic with sofas would in fact not be widened for the day?

Did they mention that you should wear your oldest clothes since you will spend most of the day on a dirty floor assembling bookshelves, unpacking boxes, and lofting beds with tools you did not even know existed? This is not a day for fashion. But not to worry: Those who look best at the start of the day will likely look worst at the end.

Did they say you would be dripping with perspiration from carrying armloads of boxes up several flights of those narrow stairs that are now going to be crowded to capacity and beyond by other (equally stressed and sweaty) parents? Did you anticipate that your son or daughter would wander away from the new dorm room within minutes of arriving, leaving you and your partner to do all of the unpacking, lofting, lifting, and organizing on your own?

NOTES: _____

_____

_____

_____

_____

_____

_____

_____

_____

_____

_____

_____

_____

_____

_____

_____

_____

_____

No?   So there has been no mention of how desirable it might be to somehow plant a trackable GPS device and a loud buzzer on your student?

Did they warn you that all of your family dysfunction would be on full display?   But don't worry, there will probably be worse going on, and at a louder decibel level, down the hall. Your job is to ignore what can be ignored, focus on what's needed, and do whatever has to be done, with as good and cheerful a spirit as you can muster!

Wait – did anyone tell you that you have three hours to get all this done? If you do not know what chaos looks like, this is it! Every college should hire large muscular handy men, professional closet organizers, and therapists to linger around each dorm on this day, roaming the halls, readily available for emergency consultations and help!

We have more war stories than you can imagine. There's the one about how we put the new mini-fridge on its side in the car, only to find that when we got to the dorm room and plugged it in, it was inoperable because the Freon had leaked out. Try finding a new mini - fridge at any local store on Freshman Move-In Day!

How about when we were told that lofting beds was a good idea, but we didn't even know what lofting was or how to do it, and had absolutely no tools to get it done? We each remember the feeling, deep in the pit of our stomachs, when we walked into the dorm room wide-eyed and realized how small the space really was. Where, in this miniscule room, were all of the items we had so thoughtfully bought and so carefully packed actually going to go? And let us know when you find a pair of scissors strong enough to cut through the cement-like plastic shells in which so many dorm supplies are packaged. It took days for those bloody cuts on our hands to heal.

One friend moved their son into a space that had been "thoroughly cleaned" – which, it turns out, meant only that the crud of decades had been polished lightly and left in its pristine cruddiness. They had to make so many trips to buy extra cleaning supplies that they ended up buying cleaning supplies to clean their cleaning supplies!

Without help, you may go into moving day as the perfect Cleaver family and yet exit as the Osbournes.

So, how does a family get ready for this craziest of days?

First, BE PREPARED! Here's how:

NOTES:

- Bring a tool kit (a large plastic baggie will suffice) that includes the items below. This is a MUST. There is nothing worse than needing one of these essentials and not having it readily available. Your kit should contain:
  - Allen wrench
  - regular wrench
  - pair of pliers
  - small hammer
  - flat-head and Phillips –head screwdrivers
  - heavy duty tape
  - black permanent marker
  - pair of strong scissors
  - several folded plastic, extra-large plastic trash bags for trash
  - anything else that you know you will need to assemble the specific items you have purchased (Be sure to read the assembly instructions BEFORE you depart!)
  - extra strength aspirin or Motrin
  - band-aids and anti-bacterial ointment. Someone WILL get cut.

- Do not forget your package inventory sheet (discussed in Chapter 8), detailing what you have packed in each box.
  - If you have followed our advice, you are making your way to your student's new home a couple of days prior to the actual date slated for move in. You will spend those days moving at a fast clip taking care of:
    - Buying school supplies, cleaning supplies, essential food and drink items (cereal, milk, soup, water, Gatorade, etc.), toiletries
    - Retrieving those items that you purchased in your home city, but are picking up at the local store (see Chapter 7) – items that were too expensive to ship
    - Picking up your shipped boxes from the Mail Room
    - Opening any necessary local accounts – at the bank, stores, or pharmacy near campus
    - Purchasing books at the Book Store or picking them up if you have pre-ordered.

NOTES: _____

_____

_____

_____

_____

_____

_____

_____

_____

_____

_____

_____

_____

_____

_____

_____

_____

_____

- No doubt about it... in the period leading up to Move-in Day, you will be at a dead run. To make your life easier during this time:
  - Dress comfortably.
  - Create a comprehensive check-off list that can serve as a running tally of your progress.
  - Dust off your sense of humor, resolve to add a big dose of patience, and you will be able to move through these days purposefully, but pleasantly.

- Be sure you know ALL details about the actual move-in process.
  - If you have ANY questions, call the Residential Life Department for answers. Don't be shy – if you are unsure about anything, call and get the information you need. It will be too late when you are in the throes of Move-in Day.
  - The most important rule for Move-In Day is NO SURPRISES.

- Develop a family plan outlining who will do what on Move-in Day. Make sure everyone agrees to the plan. Really. We mean this.
  - Emotions can run high, so determine who will be responsible for each task (e.g. Mom unpacks and organizes, Dad assembles, student sets up desk area and computer/hardware) and when.
  - You need to discuss the magnitude of the task ahead so that everyone has realistic expectations of what you will experience:
    - You will be physically and emotionally stressed, whether or not you realize it
    - The day will be total crazy chaos
    - You have a very limited amount of time to get unpacked, organized, set-up and settled in.
    - Be prepared to work feverishly and longer than you'd like.
    - One person needs to be the "quarterback," and the others need to play their respective roles, to follow the team plan.
    - Agree that the work area will be a "No Whine Zone" – you are a team with a common goal.
    - Remind each other to exercise your "Will to Chill" internally when things go crazy externally.

NOTES: _____

_____

_____

_____

_____

_____

_____

_____

_____

_____

_____

_____

_____

_____

_____

_____

_____

_____

- On Move-In Day, ARRIVE EARLY. No matter how organized you are, there will be many curveballs ahead.

- Why is the day so chaotic?
  - Your child's roommate will be moving in at the same time and he or she will also have too many belongings to assemble, unpack and organize.
  - You will be meeting new people all day.
  - You will be looking for places and things you cannot find.
  - You will be hauling boxes and gear, climbing up stairs that are teeming with others also moving their belongings.
  - You may find yourself being asked for help now and then. If so, drop what you're doing and lend a hand. There is a good chance that you will also yourself find to your surprise that you have to ask a stranger for help later on.

MAJOR PARENTS' TIP:

We hate to say it, but we've been truthful up to now, so here it is: Your student may be essentially useless on Move-in Day. He or she will be involved in all of the action going on around you and so will be constantly distracted. You will be focused on the move, while your student will be focused on everything else, in the process of breaking away and acclimating to a new home. Therefore, it is important that you have a plan that will allow you to function efficiently even when everything around you is a model of inefficiency. This is not a day for nagging, and fussing but for getting the job done. What's important to you is indeed important, but what's important to your child is also important. This should be a day of understanding.

- After carrying your boxes and stuff upstairs, what is your goal?
  - Get the bed made so you can lie down and rest. Just kidding about the rest. Sort of.
  - Unpack the boxes and hang up the clothes. If they're not unpacked now, they may not be all semester. Sad but true.
    PARENTS' TIP: For boys, put one nice suit, dress shirt, and tie into a garment bag to hang in the closet for those special occasions.
  - Assemble everything that requires it.
  - Leave the room organized and clean.
  - Add some personal touches like photos of family and friends.
  - Don't panic – if you forget something, or don't accomplish as much as you had hoped, you can always go back the next day to finish up.

NOTES: _____

_____

_____

_____

_____

_____

_____

_____

_____

_____

_____

_____

_____

_____

_____

_____

_____

_____

_____

_____

You will find that Move-in Day is not just about moving. There will be a variety of welcome and orientation activities scheduled for both students and parents – which is yet another reason why you <u>must</u> arrive early and work quickly and efficiently. Before you leave the room, be sure your student knows where you have left the pages located in the back of this book that contain critical numbers and information. Without you as an on-site reference, your child will find these pages to be essential, since they are chock- full of important information.

The "dreaded good-bye" is made a bit easier by the tightly controlled schedule in place for incoming freshmen, which distracts both parents and students from the separation anxiety they may be feeling. Colleges plan carefully and vigilantly to assimilate their new students quickly in order to minimize the emotional angst of separating from parents. Even though you may feel wistful and sad, rest assured, your student will likely have little to no problem when you leave. A whole new world is waiting. And, if you have your student fully moved in and well-organized, you will feel less anxious when you say your final – for the meantime – good bye.

If you can hold yourself together through the chaos and emotions of the day, you will have given your child a wonderful gift – a great send-off to a new life. And take heart – Parents' Weekend is right around the corner!

NOTES: _____

_____

_____

_____

_____

_____

_____

_____

_____

_____

_____

_____

_____

_____

_____

_____

_____

CHAPTER 10

THE NEW NORMAL

The trouble with the family is that the children outgrow childhood
but the parents don't outgrow parenthood.
Evan Esar

Moms and Dads, an important phase of your own lives has come to a proper close. You have worked hard, however reluctantly, to facilitate the best send-off possible for your new college student. They are now well established and living independently in their new home. You are back home now… minus one. That empty seat at the table keeps staring at you. But just remind yourself that it's currently unoccupied for all the right reasons. The family member you have so often seen at your table and around the house is now out doing what you've helped prepare him or her to do. So at least in this small regard, the world is right, and things are going just as they should.

The further good news is that you are no longer working under the urgency that propelled you over the last several months. As you reflect on where you are, realize that things have changed, and that is ok because you are now in a new phase, too – facing a "new normal." Throughout the college preparatory process, you understandably took the bull by the horns. However, now is the time for your student to squarely shoulder his or her responsibilities, and take ownership of personal choices and consequences.

While you will always be an integral part of your child's world, it is just that—his or her world. Your child is entering what is arguably the most self-defining period of life. While he or she may frequently return for advice, and just to enjoy family, it is important to learn to love life in the passenger seat of their ongoing adventure. Having labored over preparing your child for a great start at college, you have now earned the right to enjoy your new life, as well.

Now, do something for yourself. Have a personal celebration dinner. Open a great bottle of wine. Get together with friends who have been through the same thing, and now compare your stories.

NOTES: _____

_____

_____

_____

_____

_____

_____

_____

_____

_____

_____

_____

_____

_____

_____

_____

_____

_____

CHAPTER 11

WHAT WENT IN MUST COME OUT:
MOVE-IN DAY—IN REVERSE

Planning is bringing the future to the present
so you can do something about it.
Alan Lakin

What would possess us, after all of these words and actions devoted to moving IN to college, to now focus on un-doing all that you and your student have achieved? Just like that (snap!), spring break has come and gone, the freshman year has flown by and, oh-my-gosh, finals are looming. This end of the school year period of time, from spring break to the last day of school, is a very compressed, busy period for students, and the last thing on their minds is moving out of the dorm. Yet, moving out is a huge issue, especially if you live far away from home. Students have little understanding of all that needs to be done and how much time it takes to accomplish moving out of the dorm.

That's right. They've largely forgotten the massive undertaking that transpired a year prior to get them into their new college home. And in the middle of all this, they have final exams. So, how in the world can your student survive these two tasks – final exams and moving out – without a total meltdown? Our message to you is that it is imperative for parents and students early-on to develop once again a plan with specific, defined tasks and dates, together with the understanding that, while this is a student driven activity, the parent will need to provide support in certain areas.

You must keep in mind that if you and your student wait until May to deal with this process, you will have caused yourself a lot of headache and trouble. Do you really think that storage units will be available for rental at the end of the school year? Just where will you find the right sized boxes when everyone else is looking for them? Does your student realize that larger boxes are much harder to deal with than smaller ones when it comes to packing up for home?

Here are points to discuss with your student in order to formulate a plan:

NOTES: _____

_____

_____

_____

_____

_____

_____

_____

_____

_____

_____

_____

_____

_____

_____

_____

_____

_____

- Find out exactly when your student's final exams will be given, and, specifically when their last final exam will occur. Also check to see what the final move-out date is in order to determine how much time your student will have after exams are over.

- Make a reservation for your student's return trip home, keeping in mind the time it will take to pack up after exams are over. Students will need to build in time to wrap up many loose ends up such as selling books back to the bookstore, packing their final suitcases and boxes, getting boxes to storage and to shippers, etc.

- Determine how students handle summer storage if this will be an issue for your student. Upperclassmen or the Residential Life Department can be great sources of information. If most students rent a storage unit, be sure this has been done no later than spring break. If you child does not have a car, try to find one that has pick-up and delivery options.

- Help your student focus on all the items in their dorm room, and what needs to go where. They need to understand that everything can't and shouldn't be taken home with them. Every item will need to fall in one of four categories: items that stay in summer storage, items that are shipped home, items that are packed in suitcases and taken home and items that are thrown away or given away. This weeding out process needs to start EARLY.

- Obviously, not all items can be packed early, but students should determine what they will need (or not) to get through the remainder of the school year, and pack the rest as early as possible. This early organizing will be very welcome when the crunch time comes to get moved out of the dorm. When exams are over, there won't be such a daunting task ahead of the student.

- Figure out the most convenient and economical way to ship boxes home.

- Find a source for boxes, tape and shipping supplies. They can usually be purchased on line or bought locally at a hardware store, storage facility or your university co-op.

NOTES: _____

_____

_____

_____

_____

_____

_____

_____

_____

_____

_____

_____

_____

_____

_____

_____

_____

_____

- great for storage of large items such a comforters, mattress pads and pillows as well as clothing.

- Consider purchasing a clothing rack if you have a storage unit. It keeps clothes in better shape. A painter's drop cloth or sheet draped over your clothes also keeps them cleaner while in storage.

- For items that are being given away, students can call Residential Life to find out what local charity will accept (and pick up) these items.

- If you have a storage option, leave everything in storage that you won't need over the summer. There is no need to incur the expense of shipping things home that you'll be shipping right back in August, unless you'll need them over the summer.

- Encourage your student to wash all clothes, bedding, towels, etc. that will be put into summer storage. It makes economic sense to take good care of these items that they'll use for their four college years. And, they'll be glad they did when they come back and collect those items in the fall.

- When packing boxes to be shipped home, have your student take a hard look at what he or she has not used this year. Identify it so that it does not get shipped back to college next year.

- Well before move-out day, have your student find a friend with a car who can help transport his stuff to the storage unit.

- Whether storing or shipping, tell your student that large garbage bags are great for packing bedding, mattress pads, pillows and clothes.

- Remind your student that shipping can be expensive, and airlines limit the quantity and weight of luggage. So, store, pack, and ship only what will be needed for the next year. Get rid of everything else.

You know the bottom line here – have a plan and work the plan. Advance planning and removal of a significant amount of clutter from their dorm room will translate into students have a more productive study environment and frame of mind for final exams. Likewise, everything that you and your student do at this time will aid the move back to college in the fall. With this done, you can enjoy your summer!

NOTES: _____

_____

_____

_____

_____

_____

_____

_____

_____

_____

_____

_____

_____

_____

_____

_____

_____

_____

CHAPTER 12

COLLEGE VISITS

A good system shortens the road to the goal.
Orison Swelt Marden

You may be wondering why in the world we have a chapter, tucked away at the end of this book, about visiting a college campus while your student is in high school. The answer is that since our primary focus is on getting your child ready to start college on the right foot once they've been accepted, we didn't want to start the book off by digressing backwards. However, based on the approach we've taken towards getting students ready to start college, we feel we also have valuable insight and advice for parents of high school sophomores and juniors when it comes to visiting a university campus with a college bound student.

Generally, families plan college visits in one of two ways. First, they may choose to visit a large number of colleges in the same area of the country over a period of several days. This often occurs over spring or summer vacation. At each school, the family and student attend an information session at the admissions office followed by a guided tour of the campus. Then, it's off to the next place. These visits give the family an extremely brief view of the school and its surrounding community.

Another way to approach college visits is to schedule a trip to a single campus or small number of campuses in which their student is especially interested. In this situation, the family is able to take in more details of the campus beyond those of the information session and tour. This method is crucial if your student is going to apply for Early Decision or Early Action to a college, because the college visit may be the first and last time that you and your family will have an opportunity to get to know the campus and its community in depth.

It should also be noted that students are typically given an opportunity to visit a campus when they have been accepted to that college. These admitted-student weekends are highly orchestrated programs by the college to convince the student that they should attend their university. Typically, parents do not attend admitted student weekends.

NOTES: _____

_____

_____

_____

_____

_____

_____

_____

_____

_____

_____

_____

_____

_____

_____

_____

_____

_____

For any student who is unsure about which college to choose, these weekends are wonderful opportunities for students to really get a good "feel" of campus life and the personality of the place. They are well worth the investment of an airplane ticket!

∗∗∗∗∗∗∗

But let's turn our attention back to the more typical college visit, as first mentioned above, where a family visits several campuses over a period of a few days. Here are our best tips for making the most of this important trip:

- Plan your trip realistically! By that we mean to give yourself enough time to be able to take an in-depth look at each college and its surrounding community while you are there. If you literally run from campus to campus, you will have missed the point of gathering information that will help your student make a good college decision. And our experience has taught us that too many information sessions over too few days will cause the information to literally run together, resulting in questions such as, "Where were we when we saw that great dorm?" or "Which campus had the new gym facility?" So, plan carefully and thoughtfully in order to get the most out of your college trip.

- Before your go, schedule appointments for your student with anyone you and your student want to talk to during your trip, such as someone in the Admissions Office, a coach, or a professor in a particular academic department. If your child has special needs, you may want to spend time with someone in the health center or the person who deals with students with learning issues or disabilities. This can be an extremely important factor in making a college choice, so do this during your college trip if it will be relevant to your child's experience on campus.

- Bring a small spiral notebook for each family member to use. Encourage each of your group to take notes during the information session, while on the campus tour and beyond. When you get ready to leave the campus, ask everyone to write down their personal impressions of the school and the community. What caught your attention? What stood out? This will help you remember details about each campus that can easily be forgotten throughout the days ahead.

- You might decide to visit a campus (or NOT visit a campus) based on what you or your child may have heard from friends. Encourage your student not to be swayed too early in the process by one person's opinion. Approach your college visits with an open mind.

NOTES: _____

_____

_____

_____

_____

_____

_____

_____

_____

_____

_____

_____

_____

_____

_____

_____

_____

_____

- Consider how easy or difficult it is to get to a particular campus. A campus that's hours away from a major airport or that's not reachable by a non-stop flight is one of many factors to consider. Travel to more remote campuses can be quite a bit more expensive than travel to a college near a major airport. The travel issue if further complicated if the college is located in a part of the country that has severe weather issues in the winter months. Remember, your student will want to come home for holidays, and getting him or her home can be challenging as well as expensive if the campus is remote and far from your home.

- When you arrive in the town or city where the campus is located, drive around for a while in order to acquaint yourself with the community. Get out of your car and have a meal, pick up a local newspaper, talk to someone and soak it all in. Try to get a feel of the "culture" of the community. Ask your student to picture himself living there for four years.

- Once you get to the campus, drive around before the information session and tour. Begin to get a sense of the size, look, and feel of the campus.

- When you attend the session and tour, stay close to the speaker so you can hear everything that is discussed. Some sessions are crowded, and it's easy to miss out on important information if you're standing at the back of a room or at the far end of a tour group. Current students typically guide campus tours, and these are people who have a wealth of information you may not find anywhere else. So, by all means, speak up and ask questions!

- After the information session and tour, try to take time to visit the following spots if you've not already seen them:

  - the cafeteria
  - the health center
  - a typical dormitory and dorm room
  - the main library
  - athletic facilities (including those for non-athletes)
  - the campus bookstore
  - the financial aid department
  - any other place that you're curious about

NOTES: _____

_____

_____

_____

_____

_____

_____

_____

_____

_____

_____

_____

_____

_____

_____

_____

_____

_____

- If school is in session, see if your child can attend a class. Take a look at the students on campus and talk about how your student feels he could fit in there. Try to talk to students on campus about what they like and dislike about the college and the surrounding community. Ask them about non-academic activities, clubs, school spirit, etc.

- As you leave the campus and community, engage your student in a frank discussion of likes and dislikes. While your child will ultimately be the one attending college, your input is important and valuable. Keep some sort of grid or rating system for each campus with which you can compare the colleges. Allow for a good, free flow of ideas and impressions as you go on to the next campus.

The bottom line after a college visit is this – does your child think that she could see herself happily ensconced at this school in this environment, culture and climate? If so, it may be a great fit if she gains admission. But since college admission is so competitive these days, don't fall too madly in love with any one place, and don't forget to visit several campuses!

NOTES:

APPENDIX I

CRITICAL FRESHMAN DATES

Due Date for Acceptance & Tuition Deposit   _____

Due Date for Housing Forms   _____

Freshman Orientation   _____

Freshman Move-In   _____

Fall Break   _____

Parents' Weekend   _____

First Semester Final Exams   _____

Winter Break   _____

Spring Break   _____

Second Semester Final Exams   _____

Move-Out Deadline   _____

_____   _____

_____   _____

_____   _____

NOTES: _____

_____

_____

_____

_____

_____

_____

_____

_____

_____

_____

_____

_____

_____

_____

_____

_____

_____

_____

_____

APPENDIX II

CRITICAL PHONE NUMBERS FOR STUDENTS

ON CAMPUS:

Main Number of College   _____

Admissions Office   _____

Freshman Dean's Office   _____

Residential Life Office   _____

Dorm Residential Advisor   _____

Campus Shuttle   _____

Mail Center   _____

Health Center   _____

I. T. Tech Support   _____

Book Store   _____

Special Resources   _____

Athletic Dept/Coach   _____

Roommate's Cell Phone   _____

Emergency Number   _____

OFF CAMPUS:

Airline   _____

Taxi   _____

Bank   _____

Hospital   _____

Pharmacy   _____

Storage Facility   _____

Favorite Restaurants
  Name:

_____   _____

_____   _____

_____   _____

NOTES: _____

_____

_____

_____

_____

_____

_____

_____

_____

_____

_____

_____

_____

_____

_____

_____

APPENDIX III

CRITICAL PHONE NUMBERS FOR PARENTS

Main College Number   _____

Residential Advisor   _____

Health Center   _____

Roommate's Cell Phone   _____

Airline   _____

Rental Car   _____

Taxi   _____

Hotel   _____

Favorite Restaurants
  Name:

_____   _____

_____   _____

_____   _____

****

Now, share with friends what you've learned!

If you have knowledge, let other light their candles at it.
Winston Churchill

www.ingramcontent.com/pod-product-compliance
Lightning Source LLC
Chambersburg PA
CBHW081825280526
45789CB00007B/2352